942

Gift of
The Lambeau Family, Ch

MUSIC OF THE GHETTO
AND THE BIBLE

THE WORKS OF LAZARE SAMINSKY

Music of the Ghetto and the Bible
Music of Our Day

PHILOSOPHICAL AND MATHEMATICAL WORKS

The Philosophical Value of Science
The Roots and Foundations of Arithmetics
Critical Analysis of New Geometrical Conceptions
Physics and Metaphysics of Music
   (Published in part; a complete English edition in preparation)

MAJOR MUSICAL WORKS FOR THE STAGE

The Plague's Gagliarda, Opera-Ballet in one action
   First performances is New York, Paris and Vienna
   Published by Maurice Sénart, Paris
Rachel, a Biblical Ballet
   Performances in Petrograd, Paris, New York, etc.
   Published by Maurice Sénart, Paris
The Daughter of Jephtha, Cantata-Pantomime in three
   scenes
   First performances in Rome and New York
   Published by Maurice Sénart, Paris

MAJOR MUSICAL WORKS FOR THE ORCHESTRA

Second Symphony (Sénart)
   Premieres in Amsterdam and New York
Third Symphony
   Performances in Paris, New York, Moscow, Vienna, etc.
   Published by Universal Edition in Vienna
Fourth Symphony (Universal Edition)
   First performance in Berlin
Fifth Symphony (in preparation)
Ausonia, Italian Pages (Sénart)
   Premiere in Florence
To a Young World (in preparation)

MAJOR MUSICAL WORKS FOR THE VOICE AND ORCHESTRA

Litanies of Women (Sénart)
   Performances in Boston, New York, Paris, Berlin,
   Vienna, Milan, Venice, Rochester, etc.
Songs of the Russian Orient (Universal Edition)
   Performances in London, Berlin, Paris, Rome, Zurich,
   Milan, Naples, etc.
To the Mountains, Sinfonia Brevis
   For chorus and instruments, based on Navajo and
   Pueblo Indian lyrics (in preparation).

MUSIC *of the* GHETTO *and the* BIBLE

by

LAZARE SAMINSKY
Author of *Music of Our Day*

NEW YORK
BLOCH PUBLISHING COMPANY
1934

This work is dedicated to the memory of
WILLIAM I. SPIEGELBERG and LUDWIG VOGEL-
STEIN; and to CHARLES E. BLOCH, PAUL
BAERWALD, PHILIP J. GOODHART, the HON-
ORABLE IRVING LEHMAN and GERALD F.
WARBURG, men who have supported my
Hebrew musical activities in this country.

L. S.

CONTENTS

PAGE

I. THE SONG OF ZION IN EXILE 3

II. HEBREW MUSIC, PAST AND PRESENT . . 13

III. THE HEBRAÏC AND JUDAÏC SHARE IN TONAL
ART 65

IV. THE JEW IN MUSIC, PROBLEMS AND PERSON-
ALITIES 79
Classics and Iconoclasts 81
The Jewishness of Wagner 96
American Hebrew Composers . . . 112
A Russian Jewish Group 128

V. AT THE SYNAGOGUE, EAST AND WEST (THEIR
PEOPLE AND MUSICIANS) 141
Native Synagogues of the Near East . . 143
American Synagogue Music 168
A Famous Cantor 181

VI. BIBLICAL MELODY 195

VII. JEWISH FOLKSONG, ORIGINAL OR BORROWED?
(FACTS AND POLEMIC) 227

Part I

THE SONG OF ZION IN EXILE

THE SONG OF ZION IN EXILE

Hebrew music is an extraordinary texture of color and intonation; a living mirror of unusual historic sequences; an alert and teeming laboratory of tonal creeds and currents interlaced with those of other races. A study of this particular art may rightly claim universal usefulness.

The pages of Jewish musical history are as full of distant glow as a voyage to far uncharted lands, as a travel-tale of Marco Polo. Here is the story of an ancient Hebrew chant that emerges, centuries after its birth, in Milan as the great Catholic hymn *Te Deum Laudamus* of the fourth century; here, the tale of an old country-air of Bretagne finding its way into the folk-lore of Russian-Jewish sectarians; a great Beethoven quartet using the famous Jewish hymn *Kol Nidre;* the adventures of a mellow synagogal song that has lured Meyerbeer and Borodin into writing glorious pages of opera.

Jewish musical history is studded with such lore.

*　　*　　*

The many years I have spent in observing the restless flux and the most delicate mutations in Hebrew music, have failed to upset this old belief of mine.

Close communion with Jewish folksong, sacred or secular, is an indispensable stage for anyone aspiring to the distinction of a Jewish composer. Going through a strong, homogeneous, specifically concentrated racial-tonal environment, is an inescapable preliminary to the birth of Jewish cultural music.

However, at an early date I already found it necessary to segregate and to revalue more rigidly the various ground elements of Hebrew music.

"Of the Jewish musicians, who would deny that the very understanding of Jewish music's root-character is changing? Who would deny that Hebrew composition, now absorbing the folksong, is slowly abandoning the banal domestic pattern, to favor the choicest kind of folksong, and even more, the elevated type of Hebrew sacred chant with its aroma of antiquity?

"No matter how intricate and skillful the exploiting of Jewish folk-melody may be, no matter how solid personal composition built on this basis may turn out, the value of such work fluctuates between zero and a very high mark. Between gaudy mosaic, merely curious affix to Western culture, wherein, as Nietzsche says, 'alle Länder und alle Völker stecken,' and a genuine new art-thought. Between sublimated Jewish minstrelsy and noble creation of an original racial mind.

"Only through a return to its pure old font can Hebrew composition add to universal art something of undisputable worth. Only thus, a newly directed craft, a bearer of yet unknown melodic vein and harmony may emerge.

"A Jewish folksong, one of great seminal power, is grafted on the tomb of Moussorgski. He, greatest among the Russians, made this song into a jewel of cultured art, into his biblical cantata *Joshua,* the Battle-Hymn of Jericho.

"Is it not ironic justice that the tombstones of great *Jewish* composers are never illuminated by chants of their old race, by songs they did not care to learn and to emulate?" [1]

True, the Jewish composer of today either does not deserve the scorn or is beyond its reach aesthetically. The Western Hebrew musician has passed through the stage of folksong cultivation in a measure, and the East-European has tasted grandly of this travail. To probe the level and quality of racial representation that has been reached in Jewish music today, is what this *exposé* seeks to do.

* * *

The emotional tonus of the Jewish composer is marked by his tragic position, one best defined as *singing the song of Zion in exile.*

The Jewish creative musician is not always aware of his tragedy. Still, it has grown into his very flesh, and the burden ever disturbs him in some way. Anxiety in him mounts to a real alarm when he leaves the dense dwellings of East Europe or Palestine. The Hebrew composer in the Occident is a deeply troubled, a dolorous figure.

In the East the task of this particular musician is tinged with a merely mental, a technical poignancy. Within the crowded palings of his race, in whole and undisturbed communion with it, the Jewish composer

[1] Lazare Saminsky: *Hebrew Music,* Petrograd, 1914.

is to seek the most elevated, the æsthetically priceless
elements of domestic and sacred Hebrew melos; he is
then to absorb and to fuse them in tonal speech of individual casting. He must also achieve the fusion of folk-
and personal creation, a worry left far behind by other
nations.

In the West, the Hebrew composer's task is weighed
down with emotional and racial poignancy. His art-
milieu is spiritually heterogeneous and partly alien to
him. As a Jew, he is still tapping in the dark the spring-
head of a new tonal current, supposedly the domain of
his race. As a Western artist, he has already tasted of
the highest technical and creative achievement of cultured art.

The Jewish, or rather the half-Jewish, composer of the
West finds it painful, next to the impossible, to swing
naïvely into that primitive, initial stage of building
up his own people's musical foundation. No matter
how well he perceives the necessity and high value of
such work, into this labor he brings a soul split and
aggrieved.

Compared to the glorious æsthetic aspect of the West,
with its breadth of creative vision and intricate, immense technical machinery, current Jewish musical work
seems to its own standard-bearer tribal, shallow, a region of small deeds. A Jewish creative musician who
has scaled the heights of modern craft, shrinks from the
æsthetic suffocation menacing him in his own racial
task.

＊　　＊　　＊

"Singing the song of Zion in exile" brings to the Hebrew composer in the West a pathetic awareness of all the creative oddity, of all the artistic and technical penury that his course implies.

Chesterton's colorful book *The New Jerusalem* flings a curious dart at the aristocratic Jewish *habitués* of a London West End synagogue:

"We cannot help feeling that there is something a little grotesque about the Hebrew habit of putting on a top-hat as an act of worship. . . . To Western eyes, in Western conditions, there really is something inevitably fantastic about this formality of the synagogue. But we ought to remember that *we* have made the Western conditions which startle the Western eyes. . . . Europe has created the topper." [2]

And he goes on chiding the Western Jew for not throwing a loose drapery over his head in the beautiful Oriental fashion. He actually invites the Marquis of Reading and other Jewish peers to appear in such raiment in Parliament or anywhere. Evidently, Mr. Chesterton has never heard of the *talis*, the prayer-shawl used by the Jewish people at large in their synagogues.

But, of course, his contention is right. The West has discolored and distorted the very essence of Jewish habit and behavior, in religion as well as in art. An emphatically Jewish musical face encased in Western tonal frame is bizarre indeed.

The song of Zion in exile is a grotesque hybrid of

[2] G. K. Chesterton: *The New Jerusalem*, George H. Doran Company, New York.

exactly the same nature as the top-hat paraded before a Hebrew sanctuary.

But the oddity of forcing a definitely Occidental form on a racially incongruous content, is not the greatest affliction of a Hebrew composer in the West.

His profoundest despair is the absence of finality in the eternal flow of Hebrew melos. Just as the wonderful stream of ancient Hebrew biblical cantillation is thus far left without a rigid issue in the form of developed art-monuments, Jewish music as a whole still anxiously waits for a final, organic type of personal composition to take place among its peers, in the universal repository.

*   *   *

Racial blood, that maker of history, the source of our chronicle's turbulence and of its hues, is invariably stronger than a borrowed art-belief; it overcomes even indifference to one's own people's ever-present call.

The Western Jewish composer has unconsciously developed two implements of self-accommodation to the alien art of his non-Jewish neighbors. One is the mimicry of a national pose; the other, a more modest, a less discernible one, but just as insidious: the honorable attitude of leadership in the musical vanguard.

A pseudo-national mouthpiece, the voicing of a people not one's own, never rings quite true when it is listened to honestly. Schoenberg does not sound German, Mahler Czecho-Slovak, Tansman Polish, Ernest Bloch and Louis Gruenberg American, in quite the same way as do men of historical and traditional German, Czecho-

Slovak, Polish and American stock. But, of course, I am not now considering the intellectual and spiritual attitude. The attitude of cultural loyalty makes each of these men representative of his respective nation, on a par with the latter's purest blood, no matter how alien the voice of the adopted musician may seem.

As to the Americans, the eminent American critic, W. J. Henderson, has stated the case with his characteristic precision and humor:

"The creations of Jewish musicians in this country are Jewish music. Even Ernest Bloch's *America* sat down by the waters of Babylon."

Self-adaptation cloaked in an ultra-progressive pose is another sort of Jewishness made invisible—again unconsciously and through the pressure of environment.

The mimicry of modernism is a sort of Jewishness that hides its passport and screens its physiognomy. Like internationalism, modernism in music plays for the Jewish composer the part of a civic religion. It is somehow in the domain of *droits de l'homme et du citoyen*.

A modernist's guise is often an honorable but a pathetic outlet for a creative consciousness that flounders in the pain of not knowing its true racial mind; of not truly believing in the right and ability to represent what it pretends to.

In this light, modernism is a strange kind of substitution for Jewishness in music, a sort of escape from an anticipated and feared course.

But the deviation only stresses the dark longing everpresent in Hebrew music. In a frank formula it is this: to be as spontaneous, as certain and exuberantly typi-

cal, to be as racial and yet as universal, as full of elemental drive and yet possessed of the high spirituality,
as is Beethoven's *Hymn to Joy* in the *Ninth Symphony*
or Brahms' *finale*-theme in his *First Symphony;* and
to remain at the same time as Jewish as both the latter
are German.

To such a fulfillment, to an incarnation with a lofty
racial-creative mark, the song of Zion in exile aspires.
It yearns for an achievement of great value to the Jewish
people and of no lesser worth to the Universal Forum
which in the long run discards creative make-believe.

Part II
HEBREW MUSIC, PAST AND PRESENT

HEBREW MUSIC, PAST AND PRESENT

In his extraordinary travel book, Rabbi Benjamin of Tudela, who journeyed from Spain to Persia, Ceylon and the Far East, between 1160 to 1173 C.E., points to a meaningful fact. He describes the master of one of the ten Hebrew colleges in Bagdad of that time, Eleazar ben Tzemach, as "a descendant from the prophet Samuel and a man who knows the melodies that were sung in the Temple of Jerusalem during the time of its existence." [1]

This statement rings symbolically to those who know Hebrew music and its history well enough to link the living, sacred music of the Jews with their ancient Temple song.

The following sequels to Rabbi Benjamin's colorful statement should be endorsed by any learned musician of today.

Neither antiquity, nor a certain degree of authenticity can be denied the traditional Hebrew sacred chant in current temple use today. And this is particularly true of the religious song of the oldest and most secluded Oriental branches of Jewry, such as the Babylonian, Caucasian or Yemenite Jews, who for many centuries have guarded with zeal their religious customs and domestic habits.

[1] *Contemporaries of Marco Polo*, Boni & Liveright, New York.

These proud and ancient tribes, the true old Israel, have sheltered up to the present time sacred songs of extraordinary force and dignity, such as *Ani Hadal,* "Poor as I am," of the Jews from Yemen, Arabia, the most oppressed of all the Arabian Jews *(Table I, example 1)*.

"Poor as I am, my fortress and my hope is the name of the Lord! Like a flaming arrow, has pierced me the Lord, so that the pride in my heart is dead." [2]

Is it not inspiring to discover the resplendent poetical verse *Eine feste Burg,* sung in equal ecstasy by Martin Luther and by a down-trodden slave in ancient Yemen?

Another chant of great beauty, built in the same radiant, sacramental major of the old biblical melos, is the Georgian Hebrew *Shir Hashirim,* "Songs of Songs" of King Solomon, gathered by this writer from the Caucasian Jews [3] *(Table I, ex. 2)*.

Even more rugged, but no less eloquent, is the melodic bent of *Adonay melech,* "The Lord reigneth, the Lord hath reigned" of the Babylonian Jews [4] *(Table I, ex. 3)*.

But, of course, Western Jewry possesses just as old and just as fine, stately specimens of the traditional Hebrew melos. The old melody used in chanting *Geshem* or *Thal,* prayer for rain and dew, can match in its beauty any ancient song of the Hebrew Orient.

[2] A choral anthem of mine built on this song is published by the Boston Music Company.

[3] This chant in its entirety with my harmonization is among my *Six Songs of the Russian Orient,* published by the Universal Edition in Vienna in two versions, for voice with piano or with small orchestra.

[4] A. Z. Idelsohn: *Thesaurus of Oriental Hebrew Melodies,* Volume II, Benjamin Harz, Berlin-Jerusalem, 1923.

TABLE I. The Oldest Songs of Israel

Yemenite

1

A - ni ha-dal v' o - zi ir u-mig-dal

a - ni ha - dal etc

Georgian

2

Shir ha - shi - rim a - sher li - shlo - mo yi - sha - ke -

ni mi - ni - shi - kot pi - hu ki————

to - bim do - de - kha mi - ya - - - yin etc.

Babylonian

3

A - do - nay me - lech, A - do - nay ma - lach,

A - do - nay yim - loch le - o - lam va - ed

15

East European

Persian

Sh'ma Is - ra - el, A - do - nay E - lo - he - nu,

A - do - nay e - chad——

Old Ashkenazic

ve - ha - ko - ha-nim - ah——

Georgian

It - ga - dal v' it - ka - dash shme ra - ba

be - al - ma di - be - ra hi - ru - te ve - yam - lich

mal - khu - te— ve - yatz - mach

pur - ka - ne— vi - ka - reb—

me - shi - he A - men

etc.

Coda jubilans, Exodus XV, 1

a)

O - shi - ro l'A - do - nay ki - go - o go - o

b)

ha - zak, ha - zak v' nis - ha - zak—

Coda, Genesis VI, 8

v' No - - ah mo - tzo chen—

be - e - ne A - do - nay.

Yemenite

Ye - bo - re - che -cho   ve-yish - me
A - do - - - nay

re - cho   O - men.

And it is built in the noble *Æolian Mogen-Ovos*, so typical of the old Semitic chant. I have used this majestic canticle (see *Table I, ex. 4*) in my biblical ballet *Rachel* to depict Laban's and his sons' stern address to Jacob, before they know that Jacob is their kinsman.[5]

Study of the particular tonal material that was or is used by the Jewish people in their domestic life and in the synagogue makes this certain.

There exists a Jewish musical tradition. There exists a typical, inherited melodic trend that can be traced from the early remnants of Hebrew sacred song, the cantillation of the Scriptures, to the synagogal melody of the Rhineland of the eleventh century, and to the Hebrew sacred and domestic song of today.

* * *

Let us restore the picture of the religious ceremonial at the Temple of Jerusalem in the first century C.E., a picture drawn from historic evidence. We shall find

[5] Lazare Saminsky: *Lamentation de Rachel*. Editions Maurice Sénart, Paris.

there musical functions and details that are in use by the Jewry even at the present moment.

Ancient Temple ceremonial opened with the priest's reciting of the benediction, of the Ten Commandments and of the *Sh'ma Israel,* "Hear, O Israel," followed by an offering.   Then the *magrepha,* a sort of pipe-organ, played an interlude, and the priests prostrated themselves before the altar.   The trumpets sounding calls, named *tekia* and *terua,* ushered in the levites' chorus singing the Psalms or passages from the Pentateuch.[6] After renewed trumpet calls the whole people prostrated themselves, wherewith the ceremonial was ended.[7]

The purely musical elements of this ceremonial are now used by the Jewish people in almost the same manner as they were in antiquity.

At the synagogal services for *Rosh Hashanah,* the New Year, a ram's horn or *shofar,* known since the pre-Christian era, sounds the *tekia* and *terua* in exactly the same way as the one described by the Talmudists,

---

[6] In Dr. Kaufman Kohler's *The Origins of the Synagogue and the Church,* edited by Dr. H. G. Enelow, a very interesting allusion is made to the Levites, in charge of the Temple music: "Being descendants of the Northern priesthood, which no doubt came into closer contact with the Syrian or Assyrian culture than did the ones in the South, many of the Levites were more apt to cultivate and develop the art of music and song, or Psalmody itself, than were priests who had officiated at the Temple of Jerusalem."

[7] *Jewish Music* by A. Z. Idelsohn, Professor of the Hebrew Union College (Henry Holt, publishers), gives among other valuable descriptive material, many details of our ancient Temple music and an extensive bibliography pertaining to it.   In an excellent little monograph *Music in the Old Testament,* Dr. Carl Heinrich Cornill of the University of Breslau has a helpful condensed description of the biblical evidence concerning ancient Hebrew music.

commentators of the Bible, as early as the third century
C.E. In the Bible itself the New Year is called *Yom
terua*—"the day of sounding the horn."[8] The place
music held in Jewish life is portrayed in the memorable
biblical sentence: "Also in the day of your gladness,
and in your solemn days, and in the beginnings of your
months, ye shall blow with the trumpets over your burnt
offerings, and over the sacrifices of your peace offerings.[9]

Rabbi Akiba, one of the Fathers of the Synagogue,
saw and described the Temple ceremonial in the first
century C.E.

The Psalms were sung and recited in antiphonal
form: the leader, priest or levite intoned one part of
the verse, the congregation repeated it or sung the next
part.

This form of rendering the Psalms is still employed
by the Western and Eastern Jewry alike. One still finds
these forms in the *Hallel,* Psalms 113 and 118, of the
Jews of Southern Arabia or of Babylonia,[10] as well as in
the Great Synagogue of the Rue de la Victoire in Paris,
and in Temple Emanu-El of New York.

Responses and acclamations like *Hoshanah* (O
help!), *Amen* or *Hallelujah,* which like *Hallel* derive
from *Yalal, to shout,* held the same place in ancient
Hebrew worship as they hold in the present liturgy.[11]

[8] See Dr. Cyrus Adler's lucid monograph *The Shofar.* Smithsonian
Institute Report in 1892.

[9] King James' Bible, Numbers x, 10.

[10] A. Z. Idelsohn: *Thesaurus of Hebrew Oriental Melodies.*

[11] The essay of A. Lods, *Les idées des anciens israelites sur la
musique,* published in the "Journal de Psychologie," in 1926, analyzes
the racial and psychological background of the ancient Hebrew music
with acute penetration.

The cantillation of the Bible, that is, a chanting of the Scriptures known at least since the first century C.E., was a development of the public reading established in the days of Ezra the Scribe, leader of Israel after the Babylonian Captivity and restorer of Hebrew collective worship in Jerusalem, in the fifth century B.C.E. According to historians, the first reading of the Law in public took place in the autumn of 445 B.C.E., when Nehemiah was governor of Judea by mandate of Artaxerxes I, King of Persia.

The *teamim* or *neginoth,* fixed melodic motives used in the chanting of the Bible even today, are surely a transversion of those old religious songs of Israel. There is every reason to believe that the very signs, *neumes* or *nkidos,* placed over the sacred text to indicate the traditional melodic turns to be used in the chanting of a given passage, are of a hieroglyphic nature. Such signs, musical notes of antiquity, mirrored the gesture of the levite or priest who conducted the enormous Temple choirs. The officiating levite lowered or raised his hand in order to remind the choir of the melodic ups-and-downs of the chant.

The *Sh'ma Israel,* "Hear, O Israel," heard by Rabbi Akiba in the ancient Temple in the first century C.E., was recited and sung in a uniform responsive manner in Palestine and in the Diaspora. Very few local exceptions are recorded.

In some of the oldest of the *Shema,* in those, for instance, which are in use by the best preserved branches of the old Jewry, like the Persian, Babylonian or Yemenite Israelites, the melodic structure shows the great age

of these traditional synagogal songs (see *Table I,
ex. 5)*.[12]

The typical short range of these old chants reminds
one of the early church melodies such as the hymn *A
solis ortu* composed for the funeral of Charlemagne, in
the year 800 c.e.,[13] or the hymn *Iste Confessor* of Paul
the Deacon, of the Court of Charlemagne, a mutation
of the Gregorian chant of the sixth century, amazingly
similar to our own old traditional *Mi chomocho* (Who
is like unto Thee), the version sung at the High Holidays.

But after all, what is extraordinary in this interrelation? The Psalms and the biblical *Cantica* provided the basis for the early Christian liturgical song.
The oldest Christian hymn book in our possession,
Codex Alexandrinus of the fifth century, compiled for
the precentor (the leading singer-reader of the service),
contains Psalms and several *Cantica* taken from the most
poetic and spectacular passages of the Pentateuch and
of the Prophets.[14]

* * *

These ancient sacred songs of Israel, especially the
cantillation of the Bible, provided the basis for the development of Hebrew music through the age of the
Tannaim, the period of formation of the Mishna, that

[12] This melody I myself found in Southern Caucasia. As a member
of Baron de Guinsbourg's Expedition, I was given the exclusive right
to publish the gathered songs in any form.

[13] Emil Naumann: *Illustrierte Musikgeschichte,* Volume I, Chapter
VII, on early Christian hymnology. Union Deutsche Verlagsgesellshaft,
Stuttgart.

[14] Peter Wagner: *Einführung in die Gregorianische Melodien.*
Breitkopf and Haertel, Leipzig 1910.

is, the oral Talmud or interpretation of the Bible. This
was the era of the great religious academies in Sura and
Pumbedita in Babylonia, in the second and third century c.e. Beginning with the Era of the Captivity the
Babylonian Jewry became the custodian of the tradition.[15] It is important to notice that the sacerdotal order
censured every attempt to introduce into Jewish religious
and even domestic life, anything that might be a menace
to the purity of the sacred song. Instrumental and
dance music was finally prohibited on this score.[16]

The institute of *chazzanuth* or *cantorate* originated
in the first centuries c.e. as a metamorphosis of the rôle
of the reader and precentor, who chanted the scriptural
texts and the simple prayers. The cantor became an
important instrument in the development of Hebrew
sacred song through the early Middle Ages and later.
Very characteristically, some of the early Talmudic
tracts reveal the fact that as early as in the first centuries
c.e., a good cantor-reader of the Torah was expected to
possess a pleasing singing voice.

*   *   *

The Middle Ages were by no means a barren period
in Jewish musical history. The religious and social isolation of the Jewish people during the so-called Dark

[15] In his remarkable *History and Destiny of the Jews* (Viking),
Joseph Kastein describes with great clarity the cultural rôle of the
Babylonian Jewry.

[16] Marion Bauer, writer-composer, and Ethel Peyser, co-authors
of *Music Through the Ages* (Putnam), note very correctly that "the
music of the ancient Hebrews sprang not primarily as an art, but from
the soul of a people whose everyday life, nomadic or sedentary, was
religiously ordered."

Ages and their martyrdom, tended to sharpen the personalizing and the emotionalizing of Jewish music in a very stringent manner, just as it personalized and emotionalized Judaism in general.

The Middle Ages, era of the shaping of synagogal music, saw the growth of three processes that have given Hebrew sacred music their telling imprint:

a) the final formulating of its preferred modes;
b) orientalization, or rather "arabization," of the melody;
c) development of the synagogal recitative.

The Middle Ages crystallized the Jewish tonal taste and finally shaped the modes and scales that have dominated Jewish melodic creation ever since.

* * *

The cantillation of the Bible and the ritual synagogal song of the purest and oldest type gravitate to the following favorite modes:

1. The *Mogen Ovos* mode, popularly called the *Ishtabach Gust*.[17] This mode corresponds to the Æolian scale, pure or with a lowered second step, the latter being an equivalent of the Hypodorian scale of the ancient Greeks. The *Mogen Ovos* is a descendant of the

---

[17] A *mode* is a system of melodic motives unified by a gravitation to a definite tonic, note or chord. The East European *Ashkenazim*, that is, Jews of the Western descent and tradition, designated their modes somewhat crudely as *steiger*, ascension or *gust*, the latter term being a favorite with the cantors. There is a looseness in their nomenclature as they name their modes according to the titles of the traditional chants built in these modes.

old biblical motives used in the chanting of the Prophets. It gravitates to the same cadences.

Ages-old ritual chants such as *Thal,* prayer for dew, illustrated earlier (*Table I, ex. 4*), or *V'hakkohanim,* part of the *Avoda* service, sung on the Atonement Day to commemorate the service of the High Priest in ancient Jerusalem (*Table I, ex. 6*), or the *Kaddish* of the Georgian Jews (*Table I, ex. 7*), are built in the *Mogen-Ovos* mode.

16720

TABLE II. Synagogal and Chassidic Songs.

South Russian

Hal - bein ha - tu - ei - nu ka - she-leg ve - ka - tze - mer

k' mo   she - ko - siv   l' - chi nu ve - ni - vokh' ho

yoi - mar ha - shem   im   yi - hiu ha - to - ei - hem

ka - sho - nim   ka - she - leg yal - bi - nu

v' im   ya - di - mu ka - toi - lo   ka - tze - mer yi - hiu

ten

oi, zroik o - lei - nu ma - im thoi' - rim ve -

ta - ha - rei - nu ve - ta - ha - rei - nu ke - mo she-ko-siv.

Old German

2

Va - ye - chu - lu ha - sho - ma - im ve - ho - o - retz

ve - chol tze - vo - om va - ye - chal

e - lo - him ba - yom hash - vi - i me - lach - to

etc.

a - sher o - so

Traditional Ashkenazic

3

A - do - noy mo - loch ge - us lo - vesh lo - vesh A - do - noy

etc.

oz his - az - zor af tik - kon te - vel bal tim - mot——

From "V'shamru"   *L. Saminsky*

Be - ni u - ven   be - ne   Is - ra - el   os-

hi   le - o - lam os-hi - - le - o - lam

Old Eastern Ashkenazic

Is - ga - dal ve - is - ka-dash she - mei   ra - bo

Chassidic nigun   *Ascribed to Reb Nachman of Bratzlav*

Chassidic nigun   *Ascribed to the sectarians of Liady*

From "Yaaleh"   *Baruch Schorr*

Ya - a' - leh   ta - cha' - nu - ne -
nu   me - e - - rev   v'yo - vo   sha - vo - se -
nu   mi - bo—— ker

"Hayom haras olam"   *Nissan Beldzer*

Ha - yom———————— ha - ras   oi - lom
ha - yom   ya - a' - mid   ba - a - mish - pot
kol   yei - tzi - re   oi - lo - - mim   A - a - a———
a - a - a - a - ah - im   k' bo - nim   im   k'a - vo - dim,
im   ke - bo - nim   rach - mei - nu,   rach - mei - nu   ke -

ra - chem ov al bo - nim   ke -

ra - chem ov al bo - - nim.

In Baron de Guinsbourg's Ethnological Expedition, I was fortunate enough to collect, among other pearls of old Jewish melody, a chant of rare beauty, of exquisite structural and emotional purity. This *Halben chatoenu* is one of the finest *Mogen Ovos* structural types I have ever come upon (*Table II, ex. 1*).

It is interesting to discover in the traditional *Vay'-chulu hashomaim* of the Ashkenazim of mid-Europe (*Table II, ex. 2*), the source of Meyerbeer's famous Night-watchman's song from *The Huguenots* and possibly also, the source of Beethoven's Dervishes' Chorus from the *Ruins of Athens,* as well as that of Borodin's chorus of the Polovetzki night-watch from *Prince Igor.*

This is, indeed, a very curious line of inheritance. A vivifying stream of fresh, exotic color and new tonal conception, clearly issued from a Berlin synagogue frequented by the boy-prodigy Jacob Beer [18] and his pious father. This direct borrowing of Jewish songs to benefit great European conceptions was not the first of its kind. Benedetto Marcello looked for a melodic basis for his beautiful psalms in the synagogue of Venice, and more

---

[18] Meyerbeer's original patronymic was Beer; he added the name Meyer to it at the insistence of a distant relative who conditioned the bequest of his fortune to the composer upon the adopting of his name.

than a thousand years earlier, St. Ambrose of Milan and Pope Gregory the Great adapted the Hebrew cantillation of the Bible for their plain-chant.

It is *à propos* to mention here the arresting discovery of Emil Breslauer, that the *Adagio* from Beethoven's C-sharp minor quartet, op. 131, composed in 1826, contains a literal quotation of the *Kol Nidre* first phrase, with only a slight rhythmic change.[19]   It is a well-known fact that Beethoven in 1825 considered seriously the proposition of the Viennese Hebrew Community to write a festive composition.   No doubt, he tried to acquaint himself with the synagogal melodies.

It is quite possible that it was in the Vienna synagogue where Beethoven heard that fertile *Vay'chulu hashomaim* which provided the seed for his Chorus of Dervishes and for Meyerbeer's Night-watchman as well.

2.   Another dominant Hebrew tonality, the *Adonoy Moloch* mode—in popular terminology, the *Yekum Purkon gust*—corresponds to the Mixolydian scale or to a full or shortened Dorian of the early Medieval chant. It is one of the oldest Hebrew scales and it reigns preeminently in the oldest synagogal chant.   It traces its parentage to the ancient cantillation of the Pentateuch [20]

[19] Emil Breslauer: *Sind originale Synagogen-und Volks-Melodien bei den Juden geschichtlich nachweisbar?*   (Breitkopf and Haertel, Berlin, 1898).   E. Breslauer (1836-1899), music director of the Berlin Reform Congregation, makes some interesting statements, but as a whole, his little book denying to the Hebrew traditional sacred song any authenticity, contains a surprising amount of easy-minded prattle and quasi-learned make-believe.

[20] A. Z. Idelsohn proves very clearly in his *Jewish Music*, Chapter VIII, that this mode was not borrowed from the Medieval church.   Its purest form has been preserved by the ancient Yemenite Synagogue up to the present time.

and is also called the *Tefilla* mode, that of the prayer.

The tendency of this type to lapse at times into pure major should be attributed to the influence of the Minnesong on the Medieval Hebrew chant.

The ages-old *coda jubilans* traditionally concluding some fragments of the Pentateuch cantillation, used also in chanting a passage from the Book of Genesis *(Table I, ex. 8a)*, or the ancient Yemenite *Yevorechecho*, the priestly benedition *(Table I, ex. 9)*, or the traditional Ashkenazic *Adonoy moloch (Table II, ex. 3)* are all fine specimens of this type.

It is extremely significant that synagogal composers of a formal and classical mind, such as Levandowski and Sulzer, very often lapse into this *Mixolydian Adonoy moloch* mode when they try to stylize or to archaize their conception, especially in their music for the holiest of the religious festivals, *Rosh Hashanah,* the New Year, or *Yom Kippur,* the Atonement Day.

Edward Birnbaum, another famous German cantor-composer, also attributes great age and authenticity to songs of the *Adonoy moloch* type in his *Ueber den Ursprung der Tradition im Synagogengesang.*

It is just as significant that countless *V'shamru bene Israel* (And the children of Israel were commanded to keep the Sabbath holy), sung on Sabbath evening and usually built in the ordinary minor or *Mogen Ovos* minor key, turn to the solemn and radiant *Mixolydian Adonoy moloch* as soon as they reach the words *Beni u'ven bene Israel* which state that to keep the Sabbath holy is a pact between the Lord and the people of Israel.   Sometimes this change comes later, with the words *Ki sheshes yomim,* pointing to the Lord's seventh day's rest after the creation of the world.

Very manifestly, every synagogal composer, either of the Middle Ages or recent days, has felt a necessity to garb the words of this ancient and basic pact of Israel in an archaic tonal raiment. He has felt, almost invariably, that the grave and beautiful major of the *Adonoy moloch* mode is just the right tonal color for these words.

But, indeed, the classical and secular composition also knows the lure of the Mixolydian. A great example of it is the mighty Mixolydian unison in *"Brüder, überm Sternenzelt muss ein lieber Vater wohnen"* in the finale of the *Ninth Symphony.* Not even a modulation, but a sudden lapse into the Mixolydian coming in the midst of a levelled major-minor milieu, this passage injects into it a powerful ray of antiquity, almost of eternity.

In my own *V'shamru* written in the traditional *Mogen Ovos* manner, I find that I turned to the *Adonoy moloch* mode, without realizing it at the time, as soon as I reached the verse "between Me and the people of Israel" [21] (see *Table II, ex. 4*).

3. The *Aavo rabo* mode or *gust* which corresponds to the Gregorian Phrygian scale with a heightened third step, occupies a peculiar position in Jewish music. The analysis and history of this mode reveal potent influences that have deflected the melodical Jewish trend seriously, neutralized and cheapened it.

The *Aavo rabo steiger,* although the mode of many

[21] Lazare Saminsky: *Sabbath Evening Service,* Second Edition, Bloch Publishing Company, New York.

traditional synagogal songs, yet is not found in the old cantillation of the Bible. From all evidence, it has derived from Arabic and Moorish sources. This scale is identical with the so-called *Hedjaz* mode in which, for instance, is built the great Moslem hymn *Allahu akbar* (Great is the Lord) sung by the Moslem priests in calling the faithful to prayer. It is likely that the Arabs themselves assimilated this mode from the Turkoman or Mongol tribes of Middle Asia during the great Moslem conquest and have in their turn imparted this popular Oriental scale to the Jews.

During the Middle Ages the cultural life of the Jews and the Arabs of Spain and the Near East intermingled so utterly that both poetic and the musical forms of the Jewish people underwent a sharp process of orientalization.

The Arabic *Hedjaz* or Hebrew *Aavo rabo* mode, especially contagious to Oriental-Semitic races, has become the popular scale of the Oriental highway, and it has contributed greatly to the neutralizing and the degrading of all Oriental music. It has contaminated the Jewish religious melody and even more so the Jewish folksong, especially that of Eastern Europe. This mode should be dubbed the *wandering scale* [22] as one finds its stamp everywhere. In an Armenian or a Spanish church-hymn; in a Turkish roundel or an Arabian love-song; in a Rumanian plaintive ballad, a *doyna,* or in a

[22] In the chapter "Music of the Russian Orient" of my book *Music of Our Day* (Thomas Y. Crowell Company, New York), I describe the levelling influence of this "wandering scale" in the racial music of Asia Minor.

Jewish wedding dance-song from Galicia or Volynia, in Southeastern Europe.

The well-known synagogal lament, *Eli Zion,* sung in memory of the destruction of Jerusalem, is one of the typical wandering songs, although built in the harmonic minor, or, to word it in Hebrew popular terms, in the *Mi sheberach* mode.   One finds this tune enjoying also the rank of a folksong in Germany, Spain and Bohemia; it is known, too, as an old canticle *Salue mundi salutare.*[23]

Another nomadic tune, known to various chassidic Austrian circles of the early nineteenth century, emigrated to Palestine and has become a favorite folksong there under the new name, *Hava Nagila.*[24]

Still, admirable monuments of Hebrew sacred song of the *Aavo rabo* type have been bequeathed to us, particularly by the chassidic movement and by the best creative forces of the East-European *chazzanuth.*   The old Ashkenazic dirge, the *Kaddish,* that fine "canticle of mortality," to use Lawrence Gilman's beautiful description,[25] is an *Aavo rabo* structure (*Table II, ex. 5*) .

*   *   *

Among the best and the oldest representatives of Israel's melodic heritage there exist several great chants built in a mixed scale usually combining features of the

[23] Aaron Friedmann establishes, in his book *Der Synagogale Gesang,* the similarity between *Eli Zion* and the traditional church hymn *Laudate Zion.*

[24] A. Z. Idelsohn: "Musical Characteristics of East-European Folksong," *Musical Quarterly,* October 1932.

[25] Lawrence Gilman applies this admirable term to Tschaikovski's *Sixth Symphony* in his *Phases of Modern Music* (Harper).

Mi sheberach mode, that is, harmonic minor with those of the Æolian *Mogen Ovos* mode.

To this type belong two wonderful specimens of Jewish melodic genius: the well-known chant of the *Kol Nidre,* and the beautiful old Sephardic *Kaddish,* prayer for the dead, the version harmonized and orchestrated by Ravel.

Rules guiding the form of recitation and the chanting of both of these hymns are found in the written precepts of some of the leading rabbis in Rhineland and Champagne, as early as the eleventh century.

In the case of *Kol Nidre,* an established traditional melody has been known since at least the beginning of the sixteenth century. The great rabbi Joseph Karo, author of the Jewish code of civil and religious behavior, the *Shulchan Aruch* published in 1564, orders the precentor or *chazzan* to use the traditional chant only when reciting the *Kol Nidre.*[26]

* * *

Two parallel developments have laid a broad and richly colored melodic foundation for the "new" folksong of Jewry—to be born with the New Era and the Jewish emancipation. They are, on the one hand, the orientalizing process, a result of Moslem influences and, on the other, the development of the cantorial recitative and that of an improvisation which elaborated the chanting of the *piyutim,* religious poems known since early in the ninth century.

The young and dynamic New York writer, David

[26] Aaron Friedmann: *Der Synagogale Gesang,* Berlin 1904.

Ewen, points very interestingly, in his *Hebrew Music*,[27]
to the fact that the culmination of the age of the *piyutim*
is contemporary with the era of the Minnesong in Germany and of the *chant des trouvères* in France.   It is
interesting to see that in spite of the awesome isolation
of the Jewish people in the Middle Ages, one always
finds a vibration in Jewish cultural life similar and
sympathetic to the intellectual movement within Chris-
tendom.   The birth of Chassidism is but a sympathetic
wave of the same spiritual ether that underlies the Christian pietist current of the eighteenth century.

The influence of Islam is responsible for a new metric
neatness that impressed itself on the Jewish song in the
later part of the Middle Ages and helped to crystallize
the coming Jewish folksong and its forms.

One of the most beautiful later *piyutim* of the Middle
Ages is the great synagogal hymn sung on Atonement
Day, the *Unsane Tokef*.   Levandowski's choral setting
of this hymn, one of his best works, is the most popular
in synagogal use.   But Moses Milner's choral version is
music of genius; especially beautiful and original is the
choral opening and the following cantor solo.

I shall reproduce here the text of *Unsane Tokef*, so
often sung by the Jewish martyrs, and repeat the touching legend as it reads in the Hebrew *machzor*, old
prayer-book with commentaries:

> "We will celebrate the mighty holiness of this
> day for it is one of awe and terror.   Thereon is thy
> dominion exalted and thy throne is established in

[27] David Ewen: *Hebrew Music*, Bloch Publishing Company, New
York 1931.

mercy, and thou sittest thereon in truth. Verily it is thou alone who art judge and arbiter, who knowest and art witness; thou writest down and settest the seal, thou recordest and tellest; yea, thou rememberest the things forgotten. Thou unfoldest the records, and the deeds therein inscribed proclaim themselves; for lo! the seal of every man's hand is set thereto. The great trumpet is sounded; the still smaller voice is heard; the angels are dismayed; fear and trembling seize hold of them as they proclaim, Behold the Day of Judgment."

This meditation was composed, or at least reduced to its present form, by Rabbi Meshullam ben Kalonymos, who flourished in Mayence about the year 1000. There is a well-known legend as to its origin, which is recounted in a manuscript attributed to Rabbi Ephraim of Bonn, who lived in the latter part of the twelfth century. It tells of one Rabbi Ammon of Mayence, and relates how the Sovereign of that Court continually urged the Rabbi to change his faith, and how, exasperated at length by his repeated refusals, he ordered his hands and feet to be mutilated. The Festival of the New Year was then at hand, and the Rabbi, dying from the effects of his wounds, was at his own request carried into the synagogue. When the cantor was about to recite the Sanctification, Rabbi Ammon stayed him, saying, 'Pause that I may sanctify the most holy Name.' He then began the hymn *Unsane Tokef* and expired as he reached the middle of the hymn."

Not a square, not a day of that gruesome age was left unstained by the barbarian. The hapless Jew of the Dark Ages might have addressed the ferocious robber-

baron as another scourge was addressed, in the delicate
lines of a poet of today:

> "Seek not to turn all vintages to blood;
> Leave me one city, War, on a brown stream,
> The crumbling cornices, the dust, my dreams." [28]

*   *   *

In one of his essays, Francis Bacon offers consolation
of a rather grim kind but still badly needed after these
unendurable pictures of Jewish martyrdom. He unwittingly destroys the ready contrasting of the pathetic
medieval elegy, Jewish or Christian, with the hymns of
joy of the ancient Israelites and evokes the tragic passages in minor of our Old Scriptures. Glorifying ad-
versity as the ennobler of man, Bacon says with his
acute precision:

> "Prosperity is the blessing of the Old Testament;
> adversity is the blessing of the New; which carrieth
> the greater benediction, and the clearer revelation
> of God's favour. Yet even in the Old Testament,
> if you listen to David's harp, you shall hear as many
> hearse-like airs as carols; and the pencil of the Holy
> Ghost hath laboured more in describing the afflic-
> tions of Job than the felicities of Solomon." [29]

The New Era, arriving with the triumph of Protes-
tantism and the Thirty Years' War, flowing into the age
of Versailles and the French Encyclopedists, and later

[28] Pitts Sanborn: *Vie de Bordeau*, Nicolas L. Brown, Philadelphia
1916.
[29] Francis Bacon, Baron of Verulam, Viscount of St. Albans: *The
Essays or Counsels Civil and Moral*, J. M. Dent, London.

culminating in the French Revolution, brought in mighty agents that have discolored and disarrayed the stern substance of the old Hebrew music.

The downfall of the Ghetto and the regaining by Jewry of their civic and cultural rights—after a lapse of some eighteen centuries—generated a tremendous stream of civic and cultural intercourse with their neighbors. Violent assimilation, prompted by the amazing mental flexibility of the race, could not fail to follow. In both branches of Hebrew song, the sacred and the secular, a two-century period of imitation set in.

If the old Jewry was a racial and religious commonwealth, the new Israel has gradually descended to a "unity of intellectual and spiritual attitude," to use Lion Feuchtwanger's formula. Through the tragic run of the Middle Ages the Synagogue fought, just as the Church did, against domestic music, and especially, against the penetration of it into the ritual. But the Synagogue then found itself unable to stem the influx of a newly-born personal composition. The Jewish creative musician, liberated from the ritual yoke, threw himself greedily on the music of his Christian neighbors, absorbing not alone their melodic possessions but the very spirit of the Christian song, religious and secular.

For the Jewish domestic folksong this was, however, the epoch of a certain maturing, clarifying and strengthening of contour. The latter was spurred by contact with the firm rhythm of the surrounding peoples, mainly of the European Southeast and Germanic West.

Such assimilation accelerated the rhythmic sharpening in Jewish domestic song, in lullabies, love-songs, wedding dances. This process was begun earlier by the migration of the Jews from the Near East, Spanish-Moorish and Latin-Moorish regions, such as Asia Minor, Spain and Southern France, to the Germanic and Slavic East.

But for synagogal music this period was one of emasculation and of de-hebraization.

A decay of the partition that had kept Hebrew sacred music immune from the alluring poison of the Jewish domestic and alien folksong, also contributed to the establishing of an odd, baroque synagogal melos. The latter replaced the old, finely austere modal chant. Interaction between the synagogue and the new folksong brought forward a new, sharply rhythmic type of semi-religious melody as a by-product. The old table-songs, *z'miroth*, acquired a novel, highly colored tonal dress. And a fresh domain, that of *chassidic* songs, was created.

The *chassidic* or Jewish pietists' movement originated in the teaching of Israel Baal Shem-Tov, Master of the Good Name, of Galicia (1700-1760), saint and progenitor of a dynasty of *tzadikim, i.e.,* righteous men, rabbis and miracle-makers. This current was an upshot of various pantheistic and mystical Palestinian doctrines of the sixteenth century. The *chassidim,* just as the early Palestinian mystics and *cabalists* [30] (pantheists), attributed a special importance to music.

They taught that ecstasy rather than reason is the path of communion with the Almighty, that the world

[30] The doctrine of the cabalists defines the world as an emanation of God.

of melody and the world of repentance are closely allied. The *chassidim* insisted upon continuous creation of new songs, as these rejuvenate the world.

As I have already said, the "new" Jewish folksong was shaped by the orientalizing and the rhythm-forming process of the Middle Ages. But the new spiritual forces of the *chassidim* gave the reborn Jewish song its final mold. The chassidic song is marked by a peculiar color and power. Naturally, the ecstatic lyric texts of these songs account for much of their might.

The extraordinary songs ascribed to eminent chassidic *tzadikim* (saintly rabbis) are a kind of pantheist manifesto. The famous song attributed to Rabbi Levi Itzhak of Berditchev, Southwestern Ukraine (1740-1810), presents a modal pattern just as extraordinary as is its formal structure. Tonally it is a mixture of minor passages and modified Phrygian *Aavo rabo* cadences, interspersed with slips into sudden major; formally, a developed recitative, almost an *arioso* followed by a rhythmic and lively *codetta*.

"O Master of the Universe! *Aie em'tzoacha?* Where shall I seek Thee?—There is no corner bereft of Thy sacred Presence. In the East and in the West, above and below, ever Thou, Thou, Thou!" [31]

The adorable song *Ale malochim* is ascribed to another great chassidic leader, scholar and saint, Rabbi Shneur Zalman of Liadi, Lithuania (1747-1813). According to legend, it was sung by him before each

[31] My own arrangement of this beautiful song for voice and piano, entitled *The Great Rabbi's Invocation*, is published by Carl Fischer, New York.

sermon. It also is a simple pantheistic statement: "All the Angels and all the Seraphim query: Where is God? *Oi wei, l'es asser puno l'minei.* There is no place deprived of Thy blessed Presence!"

The chassidic songs without words called *nigunim,* the most popular of their kind and built almost invariably in the *Aavo rabo* mode, have more of rhythmic substance.

Of the two other chassidic melodies quoted here, *Reb Nachman's Nigum (Table II, ex. 6)* is said to be a song by Rabbi Nachman of Bratzlav (1772-1811), and *Ladier Chabǎdnitze* is a dance of the sectarians of the *chabad* creed, adherents of Rabbi Schneur Zalman *(Table II, ex. 7).* Each has as fine a melodic profile, and a rhythmic bend as emphatic, as any great folksong need have.[32]

I cannot close this chapter without describing a chassidic song of extraordinary spiritual import and very typical of the racial and religious psychology of the Jewish people.

The so-called *Kaddish* of Levi Itzhak of Berditchev is a provoking, a rather arrogant reprimand to the Almighty for His trying Israel with all sorts of reversals, blended with an appeal to the Lord's fatherhood and a reverend glorification of His Name:

"I greet Thee, O Master of Being!
   I, Levi Itzhak ben Sara of Berditchev, have come to
      Thee with a complaint.

[32] These two tunes are each arranged in a simple version for piano, in my collection *Ten Hebrew Folk-songs and Folk-dances.* Carl Fischer, New York.

What holdst Thou against Thy people of Israel?
What dost Thou desire from Thy people of Israel?
And why dost Thou oppress Thy people of
    Israel? [33]
O Father, look at all the living nations,
    the Babylonians, the Persians, the Edomites!
What do the Frenchmen say?
    —Our king is the king!
And the Englishmen, what do they say?
    —Our sovereign is the master!
And I, Levi Itzhak ben Sara of Berditchev, say:
    Isgadal v'iskadash sh'me rabo!
    *Magnified and sanctified be the name of the
    Lord.* [34]
And I, Levi Itzhak ben Sara of Berditchev say:
    Lo azus mimkomi!   I shall not stir from my
    place!
An end should there be to all this!
The suffering of Israel must terminate!
Isgadal v'iskadash sh'me rabo!
*Magnified and sanctified be the name of the
Lord!"*

It is most illuminating to find in these fiery words the
kernel of the Hebrew religio-political creed which considers the Jew a citizen of *Civitas Dei*, of God's own
republic, above all.   In this, the psychology of "Catholic
Israel"—to use the admirable description of Dr. Solomon
Schechter—is not different from the Roman Catholic

[33] *"Wos host du dich ongesetzt auf dein volk Isroel,"* in the amusing
turn of the Yiddish vernacular.

[34] In the chapter "The Kingdom of God" of his powerful book *Some
Aspects of Rabbinic Theology,* Dr. Solomon Schechter shows how the
rabbinical conception, following the direct demands of the Bible,
formed the Hebrew idea of God as a reigning power.

idea of the reigning Christ and His reigning vicars to whom every Christian owes his first allegiance.

————————

The New Era was clearly marked by the passing of the anonymous composer, creator of the old synagogal chant and the medieval folksong. This new period of acknowledged creative effort and of free creative choice was also the beginning of a surrender to alien art. The Jewish race has been gradually losing a creative position of its own.

Each of the great Hebrew composers of the New Era became a master of an imitative, levelled style: Mendelssohn—a leader of the German classical or, rather, post-classical school; Rubinstein—holder of a similar position in Russia; Meyerbeer—a grandee of the French opera, another affix to the *"empire"* of the post-Bourbon epoch.

Of course, within their reflected pattern one finds a timid gleam of racial self-assertion, one perceives broken, gentle threads of Hebrew melos. Such are the trio of the Anabaptists in Meyerbeer's *Prophet* or Marcel's *a parte* in the duel scene in *The Huguenots,* with their driving biblical and modal sternness, or the famous Night-watchman's song in the same opera—a song whose kinship with the old synagogal *V'shamru* and *Vay'chulu hashomaim* cannot be mistaken. Melodic designs such as the themes of Mendelssohn's wistful *Lied ohne Worte* in b-minor or his *Scottish Symphony* (main theme of the *allegro*) , or such designs as some of Rubinstein's *Persian Songs,* stand out in the discolored main flow. They voice an undefiled creative sanctum.

In the music of the so-called classics of the synagogue, another imitators' gallery, one finds the same troubled and lone racial islets, dotting the synagogal song of the New Era. The dignified weakness of Solomon Sulzer (1804-1890), a flabby Viennese-Jewish echo of the minor classics, is startlingly interrupted by a voice of a passed power when he suddenly enunciates his fine *En komocho bo'elim Adonoy* (None is like unto Thee, Almighty Lord) [35] in a ringing jubilant major of the biblical recitative. Louis Levandowski (1821-1894) of the square and regimented choral structures, the sub- servient understudy of the new church-composer, father of the Berlin baroque who forgot his vigorous Lutheran choral, this very Levandowski throws off his odd, bor- rowed uniform to sing on Atonement Day a mighty *Ki Keshimcho*.[36] This chant breathes the style and pathos of the religious songs of the Jewish Middle Ages, of our martyred forefathers; it echoes the terrifying yet sublime hymns that resounded in the torture chamber and at the *auto-da-fé* of the Inquisition.

Tame, sweetened are the synagogal works of the adopted Parisian, famous cantor-composer and friend of Meyerbeer, the accomplished Samuel Naumburg (1815-1880). But his *Adonoy, Adonoy, El rachum v'chanum,* "Lord, God, merciful and compassionate," [37] surprises us with racial-emotional might.

Of course, the latter synagogal music, that of the nine-

---

[35] Solomon Sulzer: *Shir Zion,* Vol. I, Vienna 1838. Sulzer's *En- Komocho,* an unaccompanied recitative, is arranged for cantor and choir in my *Holiday Services* (Bloch Publishing Co.).

[36] L. Levandowski: *Todah vesimrah,* Berlin 1882.

[37] Samuel Naumburg: *Shire Kodesh* (Chants Religieux), Paris 1864.

teenth century, knows a much stronger and a more authentic Hebrew utterance. The creation of men admirably endowed, the work of Jewish composers of sacred music with such an unerring instinct for the old synagogal style as Eliezer Gerovitch of Russia (1844-1913), or Baruch Schorr, famous Galician cantor-composer (1823-1904) and particularly, Nissan Beldzer, a man of genius, is a belated but noble and forceful reflection of our old sacred melos.

In Baruch Schorr's fine recitative that opens his *Yaale,* sung on the Eve of Atonement Day [38] (*Table II, ex. 8*), it is heartening to watch that unerring sense of Israel's true and ancient melodic style and to be lifted by the flow of its pathos. This *Yaale* has a telling kinship with the ancient Yemenite *Yevorehehah,* priestly benediction.

Nissan Spivak, nicknamed Nissié Beltzer, possibly the most gifted and inspired composer of synagogal music of the New Era and an admirable choir leader, was born in 1824 in a Lithuanian townlet. In spite of a rather poor voice, he officiated as cantor in Beltzi, a Bessarabian town. He died in 1906 at the court of the chassidic *tzadik,* the rabbi-saint of Sadigura in Galicia. His numerous works are most unfortunately in manuscript form, scattered about Eastern Europe and the United States.

As a member of Baron de Guinsbourg's Expedition, I collected among others, several sacred songs of Nissié Beltzer. I have utilized his magnificent *Av harachmim* (Father of mercy) for the chorus of Jewish martyrs

[38] Baruch Schorr: *Neginoth.* Bloch Publishing Company, New York.

marching to the *auto-da-fé,* in my opera-ballet, *The Vision of Ariel.* The lofty and pathetic text of *Av harachmim* was composed during the first crusade in 1096, famous or, rather, infamous for the terrifying massacre of the Jews in the Rhineland.

> Father of Mercy, who dwellest in high,
> Take into Thy loving fold
> With fatherly compassion
> Those who suffer for Thy glory,
> For the magnifying of Thy Holy Name.
> O Father, behold in mercy
> Thy faithful, the righteous, the pure ones.

Another creation of Beltzer's genius in his *Hayom haras olam,* a hymn sung at the Orthodox synagogues on New Year (*Table II, ex. 9*) :

> "On that day we stood before Thee and we asked: are we Thy sons or Thy slaves? . . . If we *are* Thy sons, then have pity with us, even as a father spares his children."

These quickening oases of Jewish melodic genius, that rise in spite of the levelling weight of imitation, are symptomatic and gratifying. The vitality of Israel's stem could not be more clearly manifested.

———

Renaissance is a style that couples the resurrection of an old and abandoned principle of art with detail incepted from the immediate past. Thus, for instance, the early Italian Renaissance restored to architecture the straight-line roofing and the Greek pillar supplemented with the semi-circular, column-supported arch of the

Romanesque, the rectangular or cruciform lay-out and the dome of Byzantine art, the vault-rib detail and cloister of the Gothic, the dented battlement of the Norman and the crenellated battlement of the Moor.

The Renaissance in Jewish music, a mighty current germinated at the beginning of the twentieth century and represented today by important creative forces, such as Ernest Bloch, Joseph Achron, Michael Gniéssin, Moses Milner and Alexander Krein, is no exception to the rule of renascent craft.

The direction of this Jewish musical Renaissance is a categoric and forceful return to the old Hebraic melos. The ornament of this resurrected style consists of the modal-oriental and rhythmical patterns found in the newer Jewish folksong, in its favorite melodic refrains and curves.

The return of the Jewish musician to his ages-old song, after two centuries of indifference or of frank contempt, was brought about by the renewal of a strong Palestine-ward and Zionist current in Russia in the eighties of the past century (the *Bilou* movement) and in the world-at-large by the Zionist activities under Theodor Herzl at the beginning of this century.

A collection of Jewish folksongs by S. Guinsbourg and P. Marek was published in St. Petersburg in 1901; similar work was done by Arno Nadel and Leo Wintz, editor of *Ost und West* in Germany, and particularly by Julius Engel (1868-1927), a prominent Moscow musician and critic, in Russia. These efforts are responsible for the close attention of the leading creative Jewish forces and of the Jewish musical world in general, to the great creative fertility dormant in the old Hebrew song.

In 1908 a group of young composers, disciples of Rimski-Korsakov at the St. Petersburg Conservatory, Ephraim Skliar, Michael Gniéssin, Salomo Rosovski and myself, founded the Hebrew Folksong Society which imparted to the new Jewish musical movement a wide amplitude.

The interest of the above-named group of younger composers in the music of their own race was greatly prompted by the famous words of Rimski-Korsakov: "I am very glad to see your interest in the music of your own people. The Jewish race possesses a vast melodic treasure; Jewish music is waiting for its genius."

It would be only just to note that other great musicians of broad vision have said as much. In Liszt's book on music of the gypsies one finds, in the midst of vile negation of Jewish creative gift, the following fervent dictum, its writing being prompted by Liszt's impression of Sulzer's singing at the Vienna Reform Temple:

> "*Une seule fois il nous est arrivé comme d'entre-voir et d'entr'ouïr tout ce qu'un art judaïque pour-rait devenir, si les Iraélites faisaient resplendir dans les formes inventées par leur génie asiatique, toute la pompe de leur imagination et de leurs rêves . . . Rarement il nous est arrivé d'être envahi par une émotion aussi vibrante. . . .*" [39]

[39] "Once only have we chanced to glimpse at what a Jewish (musical) art could have become, if the Israelites exercised, in forms invented by their Asiatic genius, all the splendour of their imagination and of their dreams. . . . Rarely is one overcome by an emotion so vibrant. . . ." Franz Liszt: *Des Bohémiens et de leur musique en Hongrie*. Breitkopf and Haertel, Berlin.

During the ten years of its activity, the Hebrew Folk-song Society gathered thousands of our old songs, from every corner of Russia, Lithuania and Poland. Through its emissaries, it scoured Galicia and Palestine. Hundreds of original Jewish compositions based on folksongs and harmonizations of the latter were published. The Society directed or assisted in organizing thousands of concerts in Russia, Germany and Austria. Some performing groups, born within the Folksong Society or inspired by its leadership, such as the Medvé-dieff ensemble, or the *Zimra* group, went on wide missionary errands and spread the Jewish folksong as far as Siberia in one direction and the United States in the other.

Among the most valuable and eneregtic first workers of the Society were Leo Nesviszski-Abileah, a very gifted Petrograd pianist, who later concertized and taught in Switzerland and Palestine; Israel Okuň, electrical engineer and enthusiast amateur—lover of Jewish music and for many years the executive secretary of the Society, and Zinovi Kisselhof, an indefatigable collector of folksongs.

This writer served as the first secretary of the Music Committee, in charge of all artistic activity and publication, and later, from 1909 to 1916, served almost uninterruptedly as Chairman of the Music Committee.

The lately established publication of Jewish Music in Western Europe, of the *Yuwal* and *Yibne Verlag* in Berlin, Vienna, and Tel-Aviv, Palestine, and of the *Salabert* in Paris; the activity of such Jewish forces as Erich Walter Sternberg and Alice Jacob-Loewenson in Berlin, Léon Algasi in Paris, Abram Dzimitrovski, Israel

Brandman and Joachim Stutchevski in Vienna, Castelnuovo Tedesco in Florence, Marko Rothmüller in
Zagreb, Jugoslavia; even the specifically Jewish creation
of such a major force as Ernest Bloch, can be traced to
the impetus given and the vista opened by the work of
the Hebrew Folksong Society in St. Petersburg.

*   *   *

The young composers grouped around the Folksong
Society and its branches, some twenty-five in number,
enraptured by the newly discovered folksong material
and by the creative vista opened, threw themselves indis-
criminately upon every specimen of the domestic song,
even upon the lowest type of love-song and wedding
tune; upon refrains from Goldfaden's popular operettas
down to the banal street-songs of the ghetto.   The composer greedily utilized for his newly fostered Jewish
musical idiom, every melodic pattern that could be
classed as Jewish.

But even such meager and lowly melos proved to be
an incentive to fresh creation.   In his magnificent book
on Debussy, the eminent French writer, Léon Vallas,
tells us how comparatively insignificant musical impressions, such as the Moscow gypsy songs or Javanese
rhythms, turned the creative psychology of the great
French composer.[40]

With the Jewish musician, discrimination and selection came later.   The situation was clarified and
brought to a crisis by a fierce three years' battle in the
press and at public conventions, between Julius Engel,

[40] Léon Vallas: *Claude Debussy et Son Temps*, Librairie Felix Alkan,
Paris 1932; English edition by the Oxford University Press.

a blind worshipper of the domestic Jewish song and protagonist of its cultivation, and the present writer. I insisted, just as fiercely, that the ancient religious song of Israel alone possessed real authenticity and primacy in Hebrew music, not denying, however, the æsthetic and seminal value of the lofty type of domestic folksong.[41]

This discussion evoked a decided turn to the fostering of the old Hebrew sacred melody by such leading Jewish composers as Joseph Achron, Michael Gniéssin, Alexander Krein and Solomon Rosovski.

The Jewish Ethnological Expedition of Baron Horace de Guinsbourg (1913-1916) which gathered, among other treasures of old Hebrew lore, about two thousand Jewish folksongs, religious and domestic, was led in its musical division by Julius Engel, S. Kisselhof and myself.

I was entrusted with a special mission to gather the invaluable religious songs of the Caucasian Jews. I was also chairman of a special board appointed to decipher the vast musical material gathered on gramophone rolls by the Expedition. Through this and my previous experience at the Hebrew Folksong Society, I reviewed, analyzed and appraised hundreds of Jewish religious and domestic songs.

Research coupled with controlled cultivation of the old Jewish song and of Hebraic tonal expression, has sharpened the difference between the Eastern, populist wing of the modern Jewish composers (Achron, Bloch, Gniéssin, Krein, Milner and myself), and the Western

[41] A summary of this dispute is published in the final essay of this book "Jewish Folksong, Facts and Polemic."

radical group including such men as Schoenberg, Milhaud, Gruenberg, Rathaus, Copland, Paul Pisk, Ernest Toch.

The Eastern modern forces rooted in Jewish cultural soil, in the melos of the Jewish home and synagogue, have imparted a clear and bold cut to the new secular and synagogal music of the Jews. They have also contributed original turns to the general tonal parlance of our day.

The Western rebels have accentuated their Jewish rôle in a different way: as conscious internationalists in art and conscientious objectors to any musical tradition.

In his remarkable work, *Judaism in the First Centuries of the Christian Era*,[42] Dr. George F. Moore states very penetratingly that this era of what he calls Normative Judaism, built up the Jewish national entity as a "community of observance" rather than a "community of belief."

To the picture of casting a steel-clad code of religious observance, the history of Hebrew music adds the parallel growth of a ritual of musical observance. This granite bedrock of Jewish and of early Christian music as well, consisted of biblical cantillation, responses and simple monody described in the opening chapter of this essay. It formed a basis for development.

In its broad lines the medieval scheme of Jewish musical history is an ascent from the unicolored blocks of the early, formalized hymn to melos personalized. In

[42] Harvard University Press, Cambridge, Mass. 1927.

general musical evolution this ascent corresponds to the succession of primeval, chaotic and collective tonal speech typifying a given musical culture, and the latter's organic type, the one expressed in personal accent and personal creation.[43]

There can be no doubt then as to what precisely was the springboard of Jewish musical history, and as to what was its initial material. The early Hebrew chant was subject to two thousand years of melodic vicissitude, of tortuous mutation caused by numerous influences. The neighboring East and the remote West played their part as did the murderous Crusader and the friendly Saracen, the Khazar and Tartar of the Volga steppes, and the villagers of Champagne and Provence.

My aim now is to examine the historic evidence and to try to establish how much of the authentic, ancient chant is left in the Jewish folk music bequeathed to us.

* * *

In a small monograph on Hebrew music published many years ago, I tried in the following lines to trace the historic flow of Hebrew melos:

"In reviewing the history of Hebrew music as linked with the Jewish migration, let us follow its direction from Asia Minor, Iran and Syria and along Eastern Europe toward the Danube regions, and then along the Rhine-valley toward the North-western corner of Europe. We shall then notice something remarkable. The Jewry dispersed along

[43] This aspect of the general musical history of mankind is outlined in my book *Music of Our Day*. Thomas Y. Crowell Company, New York.

this great highway assimilated the song of their neighbors less readily, the farther the Jews found themselves from their Asiatic starting point.

"The Jews absorbed the song of the Orient almost imperceptibly, and the farther one follows them in their Western movement, the easier it is to separate the authentic Hebrew melody from that adoped from surrounding peoples.

"Thus, for instance, the Israelite folksong strongly influenced by Arabic and Balkan music, that is, Turkish or Rumanian, does not sound as alien to a Jewish ear as do songs of Ukrainian origin.   This in spite of the fact that, owing to their lyric quality, minor modes and melody easily memorized, the Ukrainian tunes have become favorites with the Jewish masses.

"One may wonder even more, why do the *chassidic* melodies, manifestly transplanted to Lithuania from Galicia and Bukovina, Ukrainian lands, resemble the Ukrainian song but rarely. These *chassidic* songs, however, now and then borrow their features from the Roumanian melody. Such is the case, for instance, of the famous *Volichl* [44] found in Lubavitch, a Lithuanian townlet, residence of the great chassidic rabbi, Shneur Zalman.

"On the other hand, in the domestic music of the Persian and Georgian Jews the supposedly assimilated element cannot be easily separated from their native chant.   And this in spite of the fact that these tribes know and use the typical old synagogal recitative which never sounds alien to an Israelite, whether from the remote East or distant West.

"The fact that an alien song sheds its capacity

[44] Arranged into a piece for violin and piano by P. Lvov and published by the Jewish Folksong Society in St. Petersburg 1909.

to be absorbed by the Jew in the direction from
near-eastern Asia to the far-western corner of
Europe, cannot be explained solely by the length
of Jewish dwelling among the neighbors or by racial
kinship.

"In the Middle Ages, the forefathers of the Polish
and Lithuanian Jew lived for a long time among
the peoples of Mid-Europe, in Lorraine and the
Rhineland. Of this sojourn one finds, however, no
reflection in the Jewish folksong. On the other
hand, one cannot say with assurance that Jewry
stands in closer racial kinship to the peoples of
Iran or Georgia than it does to the Aryan races of
Western Europe. Nor can it be insisted upon that
the structure of the Jewish song has been affected
according to the degree of racial kinship of the races
that surrounded the Jews.

"I wish to avoid hasty generalization. However,
these facts warrant a conclusion that the Jewish
people are guided by a racial melodic taste of their
own. This taste makes the assimilation of alien
chants difficult in one case and facilitates it in
another.

"Sometimes the racial melodic predilection,
stable and obstinate as any other inbred feature of
a distinct people, bars assimilation of alien song
altogether. Ukrainian melodies, even those widely
spread among the Jews, have not been modified by
the latter to any marked degree; they never can be
mistaken for a Jewish song.

"If Jewry possesses a characteristic taste that
gravitates to melody of a distinct nature, could this
melody create a new art-current, if absorbed by
cultured craft? Such a thesis is being repudiated
for various reasons. Some contend that the Jewish
song in its Oriental essence, has already been

absorbed by art; that the composer has already
utilized everything that is valuable in Jewish music.
Others say that, in general, the musical content of
a folksong, Jewish or otherwise, is negligible in
comparison with the mighty cultured art of the
present day.

"Such an opinion was always that of a denational-
ized intelligentsia.   They always preach creative
exhaustion of the folk-art and are invariably put to
shame by periodic renewal of creative growth
springing from racial soil.

"Also, to know folk-art thoroughly, to grasp it
and truly to assimilate it, is not as simple as it may
appear.   Having touched the Hebrew folksong but
casually, knowing neither its true content nor its
best specimens, the musical world's 'upper layer'
still glances at the Hebrew folksong with the
haughtiness of an ignoramus.

"Cultured art always has a broader range, but it
will ever be weaker of tone and intensity than
folk-art.   But is it not just the living essence of the
latter that ever brings light and color to a culture,
rejuvenates its aging blood?

"Jewish music can still expect a new history, a
new and rich life.   Technically, but as yet super-
ficially, it has already absorbed the domestic song
of the people of Israel, and what is more important,
is gradually assimilating the fine old biblical melos.
But to master this inheritance and to enrich the
great art of humanity with eternal monuments,
is the task for a coming Hebrew composer of
genius." [45]

*   *   *

This was written twenty years ago.   One must make
allowance for the too swift and too broad inductions of

[45] Lazare Saminsky: *Hebrew Music,* Petrograd 1914.

a youth and also for the flare of an early, pugnacious nationalism. But the reasoning holds the basis for a useful discussion of the points of our present interest: the authenticity and historical continuity of the Hebrew melos.

We are obsessed once more by the question, where is one to look for the old tonal heritage of the Jewry.

It is manifest to us as it was to Rabbi Benjamin of Tudela in the twelfth century, that the most remote and secluded branches of Jewry, that is, the best preserved, are the true repository of the old Hebrew song. Therefore, any Hebrew chant or mode questioned as to its age or authenticity should be analytically compared with this old and remote Hebrew melos.

I have said earlier that the religious song of the Georgian-Caucasian, Yemenite and the Babylonian Jew, the song preserved intact for untold generations, is the touchstone of the analysis mentioned. I have also intimated that among these tribes, the Georgian Jewish is very likely the most self-contained and the purest in its Hebrew usages and ancient cultural habits that include the old religious chant.

Some details in their beautiful pronunciation of the old Hebrew language, the language of the Bible, details similar to those of the oldest Palestinian tradition, together with various other features point to a possibility that the Georgian Jews, a well preserved, sternly orthodox Jewish group, might be traced to the Babylonian Captivity. Possibly, in the first centuries C.E., perhaps earlier, they filtered through Mesopotamian plains and

Armenian mountains to the frontiers of Caucasia and farther to the north.

It is most important to notice that whereas the Hebrew Georgian tribe has adapted from the Georgians all its habits of language, dress, domestic life and notably, the domestic song—wedding songs, love tunes, etc.—it has guarded in amazing purity its old synagogal melody and also the sacred language, that of the Bible. The Georgian Hebrew traditional religious chant has absolutely nothing in common with the Georgian Orthodox Christian church song.[46]

* * *

This characteristic and amazing stability of the old Hebrew sacred chant is itself a witness to the stubbornness of the Jewish racial melodic taste. As one dissects the Georgian Jewish synagogal song thoroughly and compares it with other branches of our ancient sacred melody,[47] one is inclined to accept the main contention of the just quoted statement from my earlier book on Hebrew music.

Let us scrutinize the old *Kaddish*, prayer for the dead, of the Georgian Jews of Kutaïs, gathered by this writer in Baron de Guinsbourg's Ethnological Expedition *(Table I, ex. 7).*

Its structural pattern is the *Mogen Ovos* or the *Æolian* mode, the mode of the Prophets and also the favorite scale of the oldest and the loveliest of the Jew-

[46] See details and examples in the chapter "Music of the Russian Orient" of my book *Music of Our Day.*

[47] This analysis is made in the chapter "Native Synagogues of the Near East," in this book,

ish folksongs.   The Persian and Yemenite Jews use
this mode also for cantillating the Pentateuch, and the
East European and the Babylonian Jews fashioned upon
it their chanting of the book of Joshua.[48]

It spite of the originality of this particular *Kaddish*
and of its structural traits, the turn of its mode-forming
motives is typical of the old Hebrew synagogal recitative.   One finds this turn of the phrase in every Jewish
corner of the globe and in every period of Jewish history.

Thus both angles of our contention, that of the existence of a racial melodic taste and that of the historic
continuity of Hebrew melos, accrue strong support.

Of the ocean of facts bearing out this statement I
shall choose only two more interesting illustrations; this
essay has not the pretension of being exhaustive or scien-
tifically complete.

The traditional mode of cantillating the Pentateuch
at the Amsterdam Portuguese synagogue, a mode known
and unchanged since at least early in the seventeenth
century when it was notated, is identical with the tradition of Babylonian Jewry.   The very slight melodic deviations from the modal trunk are manifestly
a result of Western neighbors' influence in the first case,
and of Oriental proximity, in the second.[49]

The old synagogal chant *Olenu l'shabeach* (Let us
adore the ever living God) originating in the Babylonian Jewish settlements in the third century c.e., became
the death-hymn of the Jewish martyrs during the Cru-

---

[48] A. Z. Idelsohn, *Jewish Music,* Chapter III.
[49] A. Z. Idelsohn; *ibidem.*

sades, particularly in Champagne and the Rhineland. The famous melody of *Olenu* has come down to us through the oral tradition of many generations; it was notated in a comparatively late period from the traditional version of the German Ashkenazim (Western Jews).[50]

Now, this old Hebrew melody is built in the traditional synagogal *Mixolydian Adonoy-moloch* mode, and yet it bears a close analogy to various fragments of the Christian plain-chant and Minnesong of the twelfth century, a Crusaders' epoch. But after all, the Minnesong is itself a metamorphosis of the Gregorian chant which sifted from the church into domestic life. And the Gregorian chant is in its turn an issue of the old biblical cantillation.

It is clear then that, in the case of the old *Olenu,* the melodic taste of the Jewish people, in spite of the vagaries of orientalization, in spite of the falsifying pressure of Arabo-Persian, Mozarabic and other influences, adapted only that mode and melodic turn which was dear to its own obstinate racial palate; in this instance, the mode and the melodic design of the old biblical chant.

* * *

It cannot be refuted. A typical thread of Hebrew melos exists. And it undulates from the ancient Temple chant to the "long motives" [51] of the *Olenu* or *Bor'chu*

---

[50] To be found in the synagogal collection of Aaron Beer, born in 1738 in Bavaria.

[51] Medieval documents and letters of leading olden-time rabbis to their congregations often command that these two hymns be sung in a "long chant."

sung by a Rhineland chazzan in the eleventh century, to an *Av harachmim* ("Father of mercy") of the Spanish-Hebrew medieval martyrs and to Moses Milner's exquisite *El hatzipor,* one of the loftiest expressions of racial song born of our day.

In the American translation of the Talmud, edited by the great Hebrew American leader, Dr. Isaac M. Wise, the preface describes the attempts to upset and to demolish this great code of interpreted Hebrew Law. The editor lists all the destructive work of the Sadducees, the Karaites, the Roman Government, etc. Pointing to the amazing resistance of this ancient monument of Hebrew culture, the editor says: "The fate of the Talmud has been the fate of the Jews".[52]

One could as justly say that the fate of the Talmud has been the fate of the old Hebrew sacred song. Just as the People, just as its Book and its Law, the ancient Hebrew canticle has defied destruction and lived up to the prophecy of Isaiah:

> "When thou passest through the waters, I will be with thee; and through the rivers, they shall not overflow thee; when thou walkest through the fire, thou shalt not be burned; neither shall the flame kindle upon thee." [53]

[52] The Babylonian Talmud, translated into English by M. Rodkinson.

[53] Isaiah, Chapter 43, verse 2, King James' Bible.

PART III

HEBRAIC AND JUDAIC SHARE IN
TONAL ART

HEBRAIC AND JUDAIC SHARE IN TONAL ART

National music is that stage in the musical creation of a race or a people when the *conscious* work of clearing the original culture-substance from alien accretion is already achieved.

The travail of blending the folk and personal melos into a national culture is left behind. The musical genius of a given race or nation has completed its effort to reveal itself in rounded forms.

The individual composer is thus granted a tongue that he can use without effort, without embarrassment. He is given a springboard that sets him free from worries of cultural adherence.

In this respect, Jewish music is still in a rather chaotic stage; it still feels its own cultural roots tangled in the underbrush.

While unmistakably existing as building material, as tonal and historical "concrete," Jewish music is in a way only a *nascent* art. It may forever remain only this. It still but aspires to a racial-creative unity. Such unity can never properly materialize unless the wrestling of the racial and creative self results in rigid, poised form. Finality is ever the pathetic hope of all things Jewish.

*   *   *

So far, the path of individual composition which truly and forcefully represents the racial mind, has been

cut through the communion with the folksong, sacred
or domestic.   The creations of Hebrew musical art,
definite racially and the best, such as Moses Milner's
glorious choral *Unsane Tokef,* Ernest Bloch's *Shelomo,*
Alexander Krein's song-cycle *Ghazelen,* Joseph Achron's
Stempenyou-suite, Michael Gniéssin's *Rachel's Tomb,*
have grown out of clearly recognizable cells of Hebrew
folk-melos.   As I have said earlier, close communion
with the racial song is still an indispensable stage to be
passed through by every Jewish composer who aspires
to represent his people in a distinguished way.   But, of
course, this, though indispensable, is not sufficient in
itself.

Let us see what precisely lies beneath the folk-
material, what is the unseen and as yet undefined soil
that has fed, and still may feed, Hebrew tonal creation.
Also, what are the agents that disturb the homogeneity,
the directness and originality of Jewish music?   Let us
consider what chances there are for the folk-melos to
become the basis of a new valuable and unified musical
culture, instead of being "a frozen block in a flowing
stream", in the neat dictum of Jacob Wassermann.
Periodic flare-ups of the populist current are only short-
lived, disrupted vistas of a possible new era in Jewish
music.

————

Like any other manifestation of the Hebrew spirit,
Jewish music has two angles which I would name
Hebraic and Judaic.

The *Hebraic* idiom, the building substance of the

ages-old religious melos and biblical chant, the "frozen block" of Jewish music, emanates from the spiritually immovable, the rigid stem of the racial mind. The Jewish religion has not spent itself in proselytic activity and acquired no degree of universality, as have other religions. But for this very reason the Jewish "community of observance", a creed highly colored and powerfully cemented, has gathered such a tremendous racial momentum as to always remain a main-spring of racial culture. The Bible has proven this effectively.

The Hebraic tonal idiom carries in a subtle, yet stubborn way the might of a racial obsession.

These are mighty *idées-forces*: [1]

the biblical song as subconscious record of the Hebrew historic past;

the condensed power of the biblical and prophetic image still lingering in Israel's vision, the power which a mathematician would call "the potential";

the messianic expectant pride.

These *idées-forces* are ever present in the Jewish spiritual subsoil.

The other Jewish creative agent is the idiom of the folksong born in the latest ghetto; distilled from new domestic melody picked up on highways east of Suez and north of Gibraltar and of the Bosphorus; from the new chazzanuth and the chassidic song full of Slavonic and Turkish blood. This ingredient I would name Judaic. It has emanated from an alien corner, acquired

[1] This term was used by the French philosopher Alfred Fouillé, exponent of a doctrine of psychical monism.

by the Jewish racial psyche; it flows from the mental agility, the calamitous gift of alert self-adaptation to a new cultural quarter.

Thus it has become possible for the Jewish tonal mind to retain the Hebraic stem as the organ of racial-religious unity and to make the Judaic idiom reflect the temporary cultural attitude.

The old, the Hebraic tonal element is linear, seminal, full of structural potency; it hides a thematic and form-building might.   It is full of a calm old magnificence.

The new, the Judaic element is mainly a color-bearer; it is a generator of harmonic and rhythmic substances. It is fluid, expressive, episodic; it is feverishly stringent and neurotic.

The new Jewish individual composition is tempered by these two flames.

In spite of their imitative nature and timidity of racial self-assertion, there are germs of an Hebraic sort even in the Jewish classics, in Mendelssohn and Meyerbeer, in Halevi and Rubinstein.   There lurks that "soul and sage benevolence of a gazelle", as Georg Brandes adorably puts it, speaking of Heine.   There glows the same poised and sunlit turn of the spirit which one finds in the *Song of Songs* of the Georgian Jews or in that radiant biblical chant, the *coda jubilans* from the book of Genesis *V'Noah motzo chen b'ene Adonay* (And Noah found grace in the eyes of the Lord).[2]

In the best Bloch, that of the opening pages in *Israel* and of the closing section in *Shelomo,* in Milner, in

[2] See table of illustrations. I. ex. 8.

Gniéssin, in the best Achron—in his fine *Adon Olam*, for example,—[3] in Gregory Krein's *King Saul*, in Alexander Krein's *Ghazelen*, in Walter Erich Sternberg's *David and Goliath*, in Castelnuovo Tedesco's opening section of the *Dance of King David*, the Hebraic idiom whirls with greater or weaker potency.

But the creation of our Western grandees of modern music is of a definite and unmitigated Judaic essence. Not a trace of that proud and poised old melos in the masterful and harsh, temporal and domineering voices of a Schoenberg, a Gruenberg, a Milhaud.

*   *   *

Hebrew musical culture is then nurtured from these two main roots. The Judaic type is grounded in the sharply rhythmic and ultra-expressive, orientalized idiom showing an abundance of borrowed and neutralized traits. The Hebraic order is rooted in the traditional religious melos with its rich and calm ornamental recitative, with its fine major turns so characteristic of the old synagogal song.

If the creative possibilities hidden in these two springheads of Hebrew music be compared, there is no question as to which will benefit from the comparison.

The result was already clear at the first stage of conscious and artificial cultivation of the folksong.

The prevalent structure of the domestic song clings to the well-known levelled and banal pattern; the influence of the high, exquisite type of Jewish folksong over

---

[3] Joseph Achron: *Sabbath Evening Service*. Bloch Publishing Company, New York.

mass-creation is thus nearly eliminated. It is not alone the platitude of common and levelled orientalism that dampens the fine Hebraic element. It is mainly a poverty, a monotonous gaudiness of rhythm and metre, a cramped range of the domestic melos that are rudely opposed to the wealth of refrain and melodic ornament, to the variety and originality of melodic curve abundant in the old sacred recitative and its derivatives.

Æsthetic inanity and yet an irritating sharpness of the popular mode of Jewish domestic song, its rhythm, penurious in spite of its spiciness, all humps and hurdles, to say nothing of the bad handicap of assimilation, have been and will be a check to any valuable issue to grow out of the domestic, Judaic melos.

Unrestrained cultivation of the latter has already contaminated Jewish music with an unspeakable exoticism, common and shallow, which even a composer of such stature as Ernest Bloch is not always able to escape.

Alien melodic pattern and rhythm, alien proceeding and form, as well as general creative route foreign to the Hebraic chant, have served to divert the latter from the right waterway.

The very confines, hitherto set for the fostering of the domestic melos, suggest narrow scope in possible development. Whether in Rubinstein's aria of Leah from the *Maccabeans,* or Goldfaden's *Sulamith,* or Bloch's *Baal Shem* suite or in Gershwin's and Copland's Jewish-Negroid "jazzberries", or in the New York ghetto-operettas of the *Velvele eszt kompot* sort, this domain of Jewish musical culture is a *fiasco.*

Even conceptions formally and spiritually larger

result in a somewhat rickety form, hollow æsthetically, hollow racially.

Characteristic small forms of racial and æsthetical worth sway between valuable *genre* and refined *badchonship*.[4]

Many examples point to a creative superiority of the Hebraic melos, the real "potential" of a renascent tonal culture.

It is enough to take Milner's duet *Ueber die Höfen,* a picture of two *klezmorim,* pathetic, uprooted village-musicians, and to compare this alloy of valuable *genre* and elevated *badchonship* with another work of Milner, his great song *In cheïder* (a school scene), also a Jewish tonal *genre,* but one saturated with the essence of our ancient *nussach,* the temple song.

It is enough to watch the transfiguration of the entire spirit in Achron's *Stempenyu*-suite, in Bloch's *Shelomo* (the *coda*-end), in Rosovski's trio *A Chassidic Dance,* to see the swift, invigorating power of the old religious melos, when even a drop of its intonation is injected. Then one has no doubt as to what should be the dominant basis of a renascent Jewish musical culture.

In an article of mine published years ago I exclaimed with the impetuous fervor of youth:

> "Development of a Hebraic culture rooted in the pure idiom, rich with potentialities, that of our old religious melos, will free Jewish tonal thought from a creative narrowness imposed by a prevalent

---

[4] The *badchon,* Jewish wedding minstrel, popular jester and entertainer known since antiquity, was a figure of some importance in Jewish life, responsible for a very interesting poetic and musical folk-literature.

elegiac-domestic pattern. The Hebraic tonal substance will infuse into Jewish music an enchanting
and treasurable air of the ancient modes, infuse
that peculiar and manly major of our biblical
neumes, the fresh fertility of the intricate and ever
living metre of the scriptural chant.

To resurrect the Bible in music; to immerse the
whole tonal body of our art in biblical melos; to
make the biblical image and chant a driving gear
of our craft: this is the mission of the young composition of Israel."

I voiced the thought first in 1911, in lectures and
articles, but this complete statement was intended to
ingrain still more firmly the idea that a definite task
lay before the new Jewish composer. And I have joyously lived to see outstanding and leading Jewish
creators, such as Achron, Gniéssin, Krein and Rosovski
directly and others indirectly, follow this intimation
and throw themselves fervently into the newly adopted
order of musical creation.

I said further in that just quoted article:

"For thousands of years our racial soul has sheltered stubbornly some details of our ancient cult.

These are phenomena of the same order:

the enchanting rite of *M'chadeshn die levoneh,*
consecrating the new moon, a usage still living in
the orthodox East European Jewish village, a rite
breathing the air of ancient nomadic and pagan
Semitic dwellings;

Thal and *Geshem,* the beautiful chants that for
ages have translated musically the pagan prayers
for dew and rain;

the *Havdala,* the blessing of the fire on Saturday

evening, at the moment of the departure of the Sabbath and of the rekindling of light, after a whole day's lapse;

the translucent Georgian Hebrew "Song of Songs", *Shir hashirim,* on which the glow of a golden noon of old Palestine of the Kings, rests like the calm of eternity.

These are basic obsessions of a racial mind which neither a highway-begotten, flat orientalism, nor the pressure of near-by Aryan culture can level or extinguish.

In the new Russian art, especially that of Rimski-Korsakov, it has transpired that an assimilated layer of Christian features grafted on a musical culture, screens a beautiful pagan stratum.

New Hebrew effort is destined to show:

that beneath the sorrowful and humble layer of Jewish domestic song, borrowd from Christian and Aryan sources, a mighty, monochrome, life-bearing ore of luminous biblical melos is to be found;

that the froth and dregs of the so called Jewish folk-music, picked up in the bazaar of the Orient and the street-gutter of the Occident, have darkened and disfigured the noble countenance of Hebrew musical art;

that the root-character of Jewish music harbors no exotic and expressive platitude; it bears a mark of poise, austerity and majesty, all the traits of cultural greatness." [5]

* * *

I now come back to the initial query as to the heterogeneous principles that distort the body of Jewish

[5] Lazare Saminsky: "Hebrew element in tonal art," *Novyi Voskhod* (Renaissance), Petrograd 1917.

music, an organism undergoing a fresh reorganization under duresss.

I have already shown, in the opening chapter of this book, that the basic tragedy of the Jewish composer lies in his *singing the song of Zion in exile*.

The composer must travail until he recovers the true voice of his race, reflected in the old traditional canticle. Then this rigid and manly though primitive style is to be coordinated with the high and alien technical culture that surrounds him. Also, he is to fight off the shallow exotic accretion that has grown to be Israel's ghetto-music. But it is necessary to note that Oriental descent has not wholly condemned Jewish music to that contemplative and verbose, ornate and melancholy preciosity which seems to have become the official style of various cultures, the Russian musical art, for instance. The formal and rhythmic mind of the Hebrew race has a taste for neatness of line and for structural order which seem to be the patrimony of the Western man.

I also said in my former article that "to coordinate all creative possibilities hidden in Hebrew melos with the great achievements of Western culture, and to weld them into a new oneness, the work of generations must flow under. Then the conflicting spiritual urges tossing the Jewish composer here and there, will be blent in harmony, and the multiform riverbeds of Jewish art-thought will converge."

But the defining of the Hebrew share in musical art oversteps by far the confines of a purely Jewish problem. I now touch the sore point of Western art.

It was not a whim of history to have kept like a lash

over the European musical milieu—and for so many
decades—the famous diatribes of Wagner and of Stewart
Houston Chamberlain; the malevolent elegies singing
the incapacity of the Jews to create original music, bewailing the judaization of pure Aryan art, the contam-
inating of the latter with a spirit exotic and commercial,
and so on.

It is true that the paths of Jewish musical work are
illumined not only by the venomous, evil torch of Wagner's and Chamberlain's dissertations but also by the
loving light of Rimski-Korsakov who believed that the
Jewish people is yet to create an original, glorious
musical culture.

After all, "Jewishness", that is, a peculiar outlandish
strain, is grafted on the body of Western music much
less by Mendelssohn and Rubinstein, the apostles of
classicism who have drowned their Jewishness in a froz-
en post-classical cyclopean style, than by others, by
"Aryans,"—Liszt, for example.   In Russian music
Glinka, Moussorgski and Rimski-Korsakov, composers
of pure Slavic blood, are also infinitely more exotic than
Mendelssohn and Rubinstein.   And they were precisely
the ones to "poison" their national music with the
seeds of "exoticism".

However, the main angle of the Jewish share in music
is very far from the just quoted outline, friendly or
inimical.

The problem of "Jewishness in music" can be seen
only in the light of the possibilities of Hebrew musical
culture described earlier.

We have come to realize that the Jewish people *did not* judaize the "Aryan-pure" music of the West. Just the opposite, Jewish music has been itself "aryanized" or "contaminated", partly europeanized, partly orientalized in the Exile. The mission of a renascent Jewish music is a return to its pure font, to the ancient majestic modes, to the structure of its own aboriginal religious chant which, as the historians insist, was mortar for the early Christian church song.

Owing to an ultra-refined, complex and crushing Western technical culture, in truth, a despotic musical technocracy, our present tonal civilization has blundered far away from its own ancient modal mainspring.

Personal creation and folk-art have long since converged their channels, levelled and bled one another. We are drifting into the *impasse* of an anemic and wingless city-art.

Among the races with a sharply concentrated musical-cultural energy, the Jewish people is one of the very few still to preserve a living tie with ancient modal roots of both Jewish and Christian music. A return to that old font would reshape anew the tonal horizon of the West. Possibly, it is a missionary task for the new Jewish music—to help in restoring the ancient water-way of our tonal civilization.

Such a by-rôle of Hebrew musical renaissance would be a noble and useful *"hebraization"* of the tonal West.

Thus the ends of Hebrew art may acquire a universal range: the task of helping to restore and reunite the common tonal creed of humanity.[6]   A synthesis, where the very problem, the accursed problem of "Jewishness in music," would vanish.

*   *   *

This *exposé* has taken up the Hebrew share in music as seen in relation to a changing tonal world. There is also a positive expectancy as to the emerging of a valuable Hebrew part in musical culture.

In addition to all we know of the synagogue as the treasure-cache of the immortal religious song of Israel, as the ever-living source of original musical creation, we must point to the rôle of Palestine in Jewish music.

Whether in the past, as the land of the cabalist mystical song, the land of *L'cho dodi*,[7] or in the present, as the country of the inspired Yemenite dance-songs and of the workingmen's *Chalutzim* tunes [8] which have come to a higher and yet higher elevation, Palestine has remained an active subsoil of Jewish music.

These two realms have then never failed, either as a repository of past and yet living cultural wealth, or as a sanctuary of our creative hope: the Synagogue and the Land of Israel.

[6] In the chapter "The tonal language of our time" of my book, *Music of Our Day*, I develop this idea of a tonal restoration in detail.

[7] This famous Sabbath hymn originated in the Palestinian city of Safed, in the sixteenth century, under the influence of Rabbi Isaac Lourié, the pantheist theologian.

[8] In the collection of new Palestinian songs gathered enthusiastically by A. W. Binder, the New York composer (Bloch Publishing Company), we find songs of great loveliness.

PART IV

THE JEW IN MUSIC, PROBLEMS AND
PERSONALITIES

Classics and Iconoclasts
The Jewishness of Wagner
Hebrew American Composers
A Russian Jewish Group

CLASSICS AND ICONOCLASTS

I remember vividly the year 1909 and the grief of a young, flaming student of Saint Petersburg Conservatory. It was the year of Felix Mendelssohn's hundredth birthday-anniversary. The god of generations had been accorded a miserable, perfunctory and off-hand remembrance. And the sad jubilee was further deadened by the usual idiocies indispensable to this sort of festivity. Cheerless mummies such as Mendelssohn's *Lorelei,* were exhumed and vast auditoriums punished with the agony of interminable and the worst of Mendelssohn's oratorios.

Now, why is it that a composer of genius who brought the instrumental form to the highest perfection, created an individual pianistic style, gave life to orchestral sea-painting of beauty and originality such as the prelude to *Meeresstille und glückliche Fahrt,* is now little less than forgotten, practically on the dead list?

Why is it that the grip of so extraordinary a master is restricted to only a few of his works?

The inconsequentialities and absurdities of Mendelssohn's life-flow are well known. A grandson of Moses Mendelssohn, great Hebrew scholar, thinker and leader of the German Jewry, little Felix began his career with being baptized, a decision, of course, of his rich and socially renowned parents.

The wind of the French Revolution, still fresh, followed by the typhoon of Napoleonic wars, had emancipated the German Jewry politically; the already existent thirst for assimilation was sharply accentuated.

A member of the Berlin aristocracy of intellect, a nursling of Zoelter, director of the Berlin *Sing-Akademie,* and a devotee of Goethe, young Mendelssohn was swiftly immersed in and bewitched forever by the staid classical German cult that emulated the cool, finished form of antique art.   He never did change, for his creative taste froze and shrunk at once.

It was a practical joke, on history's part, to "elevate" the son of an impatient, nervous, ecstatic people to a peerage in an art-realm artificially cooled and hellenized. To transform a man, whose family-tree had but recently been dug up from a ghetto-lane, into the perfect master and the last molder of a great epoch of German art.

But such play of history ever invites a lame ending.

The true kernel of Mendelssohn's creative soul was as little German, and as typically and beautifully Jewish, as was his sensitive wistful face, his mien, his peculiar lyricism.   This last trait of Mendelssohn's music resembles the lyricism of Chopin, Schumann or Glinka as little as the Jew resembles a Pole, a German or a Russian.

In spite of an enormous pile of Mendelssohn's work, definitely stamped with a musty sort of Germanism, one cannot be mistaken as to the race of the composer when at his best.   One is quite sure of the ancestry of the *allegro* from the violin concerto, or of the main theme in the *Scottish Symphony* or of "Hear, O Israel" from *Elijah,* or of the b-minor *Lied ohne Worte.*

This music has the typical *timbre* of racial sorrow; it cannot possibly be anything but Jewish music. For a singer of racial elegies to turn priest of a deliberately collected, frigid style, was to injure his true creative self forever.

*   *   *

If a name were given to a man not at the beginning but at the end of his life to sum it up, Meyerbeer would, perhaps, have a greater claim to the name Felix than even Mendelssohn had. He was the member of a most lovable, highly cultured and dignified Jewish family of Berlin. He was the heir to three great fortunes, his father's (Hertz Beer), his mother's and his distant relative's whose patronymic Meyer he amalgamated with his own.

Like Mendelssohn, he received an excellent education which helped his career enormously. His married life was cloudless, his artistic pursuits fabulously fortunate.

Three great European nations considered Meyerbeer their own. His first great success, the opera *Il Crociato* (The Crusader) made his name familiar in Italy. Germany insisted on owning Meyerbeer because of his birthplace and education. In spite of enraged protest from Schumann and Wagner, Meyerbeer's operas had an unimpeded triumph in Germany. And up to his last day he remained *Generalmusikdirektor* to the King of Prussia.

History of music considers Meyerbeer the creator of the French grand opera, and the *Huguenots* its classical example.   France and Paris, which Meyerbeer loved more than any other of his places of residence, was really his second fatherland.   Paris, the site of his fabulous triumphs, was the focal spot whence the most glittering rays of his glory took on their run.   True, as Heine maliciously says, he himself was the best conductor of Meyerbeer's glory.   But his ways of helping on artistic success—among them sending presents to the *tenore di grazia* or the first flute, to coax them into careful study of their parts—these methods are touching and naïve, in comparison with the naked insolence and loud swash-bucklery of today's publicity.

But the same traits of Meyerbeer's gift and of his work that created this glittering life-course, decolored and narrowed down—into an almost unfair shrinkage—the posthumous history of Meyerbeer's creation.

One cannot even grant that the *musicus ordinaris* is sufficiently aware of Meyerbeer's rôle as the forerunner of Wagner and of some of the other great men, in orchestral and operatic composition.   No less than Weber, Meyerbeer revolutionized the orchestral writing of the nineteenth century.

His mighty massed sonorities, his use of the woodwind and new ways of orchestral doubling more than anything else paved the foundation for Wagner's new orchestra.   And the meager, yet amazingly potent ensemble that accompanies Marcel's recital of the battle of La Rochelle in the *Huguenots*—piccolo, contrabasses pizzicati and kettle-drums—is the unrecognized parent of the new small orchestra color-schemes.   Parent of those delicious and distinct combinations that dot the scores of *Aïda* and *Carmen* and have lived to germinate the "chamber orchestra" or the "soloists' orchestra" of Schoenberg's *Pierrot Lunaire* and Stravinski's *Histoire du Soldat,* with Mahler's wonderful color-clusters from *Lied von der Erde,* as a bridge.

Meyerbeer created the historic opera, built up an admirable art of tonal characterization, gave life to fresh operatic concepts. His amazing tonal-scenic ideas, his musical molding of massed stage-movement taught musical handling of the mass-scenes to Wagner, Moussorgski, Bizet and Verdi.

The magnificent quarrelling choruses of Protestant and Catholic crowds in the third action of the *Huguenots* are lawful parents of numerous famed operatic ensembles. Of the *finale* from the second action of the *Mastersingers;* of the opening people's scene and the popular uprising (the camp of the Impostor, in Kromy) from *Boris;* of the cigarette-factory girls' battle in *Carmen.* Even the night-watchman from the *Mastersingers,* one of Wagner's loveliest figures, is none other than the same quaint official from the *Huguenots,* calmly pocketed by Wagner. And we know how well Wagner repaid Meyerbeer for the present.

It is true, however, that in managing the masses, that is, as far as the stage handling is concerned, Wagner was a poor pupil of Meyerbeer. With the exception of the finale of the second action in the *Mastersingers,* nobody ever understands what is happening in any stage scene of Wagner, not even in the glorious first action of *Lohengrin.* And yet the latter is of divine clarity in comparison with the scenic *abracadabra* and the poetic muddle of the *Nibelungen*.   Of the great masters of opera no one except Bizet in *Carmen* was ever able to match Meyerbeer's lucid operatic gift, his genius for presenting a dramatic conflict with superb visual clarity, with every scenic cog and curb transparent.

*   *   *

Meyerbeer, blessed with the same kind of external felicity as Mendelssohn, was bound, by the nature of things, to share in the same shocking oblivion and in the same creative tragedy which, happily for them, neither was aware, would come about.

The twofold root of both composers' æsthetical undoing is only too obvious.

The curse of such felicity is voiced in Goethe's classical dictum.   *"Der nie sein Brot mit Trähnen asz, nie die kummervollen Nächte auf seinem Bette weinend sasz"* . . . the one "who has never eaten his bread with tears, has never sat up sorrowful nights crying," will not reach the depths of true art.   That is, of art conceived in active compassion, in the knowing of the sting of loneliness, in a probing of human misery.

Historically, both Meyerbeer and Mendelssohn have paid the toll of being brilliant builders of an imitative art.   Stepsons of German classicism and French opera, they have paid for ignoring the channels assigned to them by their own race.   One cannot be a mouthpiece of two or three nations at the same time without suffering from confusion, misapplication and futility.

The rich flow of Mendelssohn's and Meyerbeer's creation, the magnificence of their invention went into the forging of purely European, purely "Aryan" forms, instrumental in one case, operatic in the other. Both composers were mere hammers in the hand of a regional art, *nothing else;* when the work was over, the hammer was unceremoniously tossed aside.

European art, at the hand of its great standard-bearers, Schumann and Wagner, has paid Meyerbeer for his great labor with contempt, with persecution. *"Der Jude kann nur nachkünsteln, nicht wirklich redend dichten"*—"The Jew can only mimic, not really create."

The most conspicuous word said of Meyerbeer, more remembered than anything else, is that he is revoltingly emphatic, loud-hued, and multicolored—a German, a Frenchman and an Italian, all in one; that his dramatic instinct is shallow, his creation full of tinsel and false pathos.

"Meyerbeer has bared and exhibited his heart; behold, it is empty." Thus writes Schumann of the *Huguenots.*

Meyerbeer possessed everything that could have made him a great composer in the Hebraic medium. He has risen no higher than brilliant imitation, and his case is even more poignant that Mendelssohn's. For Meyerbeer was the member of a family deeply devoted to Judaism. His father, Jacob Hertz Beer, established a Reform Synagogue in his own house, and the boy Meyerbeer composed music for the services. Young Jacob Meyerbeer himself was passionately attached to his race. He is known to have wept when told of the spiteful word of Rossini, loudly envious of Meyerbeer's success: "I do not write any more operas as I am waiting for the Jews to finish their *shabash*." However, the duplicity of Wagner who begged favors of Meyerbeer, letters of recommendation, etc., and at the same time slandered him in *anonymous* articles, provoked from Meyerbeer nothing but a grimace of disgust and a shrug of shoulder. He never spoke of Wagner.[1]

Recall those rare moments of Meyerbeer's creation, such as the anabaptists' trio from *The Prophet,* Marcel's *a parte* in the duel scene from the *Huguenots* and the night-guard's arioso, with their true breath of Hebraic melos. Follow through and you will sorrow over those most beautiful and lasting moments of his life-work. They make the grim drama of the great Jewish composer only too transparent. Here is a carrier of original art-potentiality never to rise; a toiler in a language and a form never to carry weight with either his mother-race or the nation he clings to.

Meyerbeer, the great inventor and genius of the stage, creator of the historic opera, a tremendous musical force, scion of a family of high intellectual attainment and deeply attached to their race, was the very man to create a great Jewish opera, just as Mendelssohn's natural bent should have made him the builder of a Jewish symphony.

But they scarcely had an inkling of what ailed them.

[1] "The documents we possess prove beyond question that both at Dresden and at Berlin it was a letter of warm recommendation from Meyerbeer that finally determined the acceptance of the two operas (Wagner's *Rienzi* and the *Flying Dutchman*) . . . It is impossible to acquit Wagner of a certain amount of double dealing with regard to Meyerbeer." Thus writes the eminent critic and best authority on Wagner, Ernest Newman, in his *The Life of Richard Wagner* (Knopf).

They never knew that no matter how attractive their speech might be at times, they spoke an "alien tongue."

"Wir sprechen ja eine fremde Sprache," said Mahler to his friend in a poignant moment, in an awareness of the inbred ricket in his colossal forms. It is bitter to realize that Jewish music has done little else in generations than toil over an "alien speech"; that great Jewish creators, heroes of this sad travail, have not been truly precious to the Jewish people nor any other.

*   *   *

The famous Petrograd critic and composer, and also a notorious antisemite, Alexandre Siérov, called Rubinstein "Antosha *Rebenstein,*" mocking the word *rebe,* that is, rabbi in the Jewish vernacular. And the Petrograd Imperial Conservatory of Music, which Anton Rubinstein founded, Siérov dubbed "the synagogue."

History has bestowed on Rubinstein another name: that of the creator of cultured music in Russia. He is the founder of the Russian Imperial Musical Society that covered the land with a net of conservatories, music schools and concert organizations; he is also author of the first Russian symphonies. The well-known Russian pianist, Anatole Drosdov, called Rubinstein, very rightly indeed, Peter the Great of Russian music.

In spite of his own unbending conservatism, Rubinstein, an artist and man of great nobility, vision and generosity, fostered the performance of the "radical" works of his day, compositions by Rimski-Korsakov, Tschaikovski and Glazounov who highly revered him and were true to his memory.

To this great son of Russia her people erected no monuments. And the Jewish people had, alas, no reason for doing so. The vigorous native gift of Rubinstein was unfortunately served by a typical early Russian amateur training, a dulled self-critical sense, a blind wholesale worship of the German classics, an obnoxious eclecticism of taste. Rubinstein's creative self definitely clung to the Orient; his gift for subtle tonal exoticism was inbred. This is clearly revealed in his *Persian Songs*—some of them enchanting—in the *Chorus of Semites* from his oratorio *The Tower of Babel,* in some excerpts from the *Maccabeans,* in various pages of genius from his opera *The Demon.* Yet he drowned this fine and individual perception in the laboring over cyclopean forms of third rate German make, over swampy oratorios and operas.

The Hebrew tonal spark in Rubinstein's creation is interesting to follow.

The famous aria "Sound the tympans" sung by Leah, mother of Judas Maccabeus in Rubinstein's oratorio, is a subconscious reproduction of a Jewish folksong: a melody of the *chassidim* of Berditchev, an important Jewish industrial town of Southern Russia, where Rubinstein was born and passed his childhood. Incidentally, it is to this very city that Honoré de Balzac came to marry the Countess Eva Ganska, after having waited politely twenty years for the passing of her husband.

One of the phonograms which I had deciphered when working for the Baron Horace de Guinsbourg's Expedition, is an almost exact copy of Leah's aria rightly con-

sidered a strong manifestation of Rubinstein's hebraism.
Other distinctly Hebraic phenomena in Rubinstein's
music point also to latent racial powers in Rubinstein's great and elemental creative talent. I have in
mind his majestic and sudden major turns reminiscent
of scriptural cantillation, and a deep-seated leaning to
stately biblical subjects.

However, he took to the road of Meyerbeer and Mendelssohn, to the inadventurous route of a Jewish
"classic." Another glowing gift was spent on a task useless to either German or Russian, or, indeed, to Jewish
art; spent on transplanting the style of the epigons of
German classicism into Russian soil. A very poor rôle
indeed, for a contemporary of the glowing activity of
Borodin, Moussorgski and Rimski-Korsakov.

* * *

The part played by the Jewish classic is as clear as it
is pathetic. The less definite rôle of the late Jewish icon-
oclast is distressing in a much more involved and a
stranger way.

Mahler, Schoenberg, Alexander Krein and the minor
pathbreakers, such as Darius Milhaud or Kurt Weil,
play, one feels, some sort of a Jewish part. It is rather
difficult to extricate this part from the jumble of æsthetical stratagems that prompt these men's musical doings.

Boris de Schloezer says very rightly that all Jewish
composers have definite and typical traits in common:

> "Lorsque on étudie l'œuvre des compositeurs
> d'origine juive—de Mendelssohn a nos jours, par
> exemple—et surtout des plus éminents parmi nos

*contemporains, on constate l'éxistence de certains
traits communs qui se retrouvent chez Alexandre
Krein en Russie, chez Ernest Bloch aux Etats Unis,
chez Arnold Schoenberg en Autriche, chez Darius
Milhaud en France, et qui suggèrent l'idée d'une
vague parenté spirituelle entre ces artistes dont les
personalités apparaissent néanmoins si différentes.
Tous quatre en effet (et on pourrait allonger la
liste) sont des expressionistes, dont la musique est
profondément saturée de psychologie; ce sont des
musiciens subjectifs, des poètes lyriques dont l'art
est un épanchement et une confession passionnée,
souvent violent, exasperée, non sans une certaine
éxageration déclamatoire, théatrale et parfois aussi
sentimentale."* [2]

The description is correct indeed, but it strikes solely
at the generalities of a racial psychology. It portrays
the emotional type of the present Jewish composer, not
the interracial æsthetic rôle played by the Jewish icono-
clast as such.

This rôle has two keen edges that expose the Jewish
soldier fighting in the red musical phalanx to the blessings of the believer and the anathemas of the adversary.

[2] "As one studies the work of composers of Jewish origin—from
Mendelssohn down to our day, for example—one establishes the existence of certain common traits to be found in Alexander Krein of
Russia, in Ernest Bloch of the United States, in Arnold Schoenberg
of Austria, in Darius Milhaud of France,—traits that suggest a vague
spiritual parentage between these artists whose personalities seem,
however, so different. All four of them (and one could extend the
list) are expressionists, whose music is deeply saturated with psychology; they are subjective musicians, lyric poets whose art is an
effusion, a passionate confession often violent, exasperated, not without a certain declamatory, theatrical exaggeration, often also sentimental." Boris de Schloezer: *Darius Milhaud* (La Revue Musicale
1925).

A leader is certainly not the man who understates his cause, least of all, a Jewish leader. Bitter overstress of his art-creed is what makes the Jewish modernist composer a keen participant and, very often, a commander in radical tonal thought. Over-emphasis is the blessing and the curse of any representative of a neurotic race; this trait shows virulently in any type of composition, whether in the ultra-classical trend of a Mendelssohn, or the ultra-chromatic of a Schoenberg.

Premier leader of today's tonal radicalism, Schoenberg has touched the summit of stringent inquiry into and negation of the art-standards of the past. His dogmatic and speculative revolt against traditional form attains the pitch of one possessed. But the elevation of his detached artistry cannot fail to inspire a deep interest in his work and a deep respect for the man.

Because of their corrosive acid, Schoenberg's concepts have had possibly a mightier grip on the younger creative forces of our day than even those of Strauss and Stravinski.

There is something of a saintliness in Schoenberg's frantic defense of a cruelly uncomfortable, cruelly aloof creative position. And certainly those who speak of commercial art with a glance toward the Jewish phalanx, should be just enough to pit first the martyrdom of a Schoenberg against the profitable trade and shrewd welfare of a Strauss and a Stravinski.

In this suffering for a creed, in this wonderful impecuniousness and spiritual chastity, Schoenberg is only another example of moral greatness that marks many great Jewish figures: Spinoza and Karl Marx, who accepted abject poverty and exile for the sake of their teaching and their mental freedom; Jesus of Nazareth, for that matter!

Two outstanding American writers on music have had the sensitiveness to register the peculiar epic suffering, a singular tragic distinction in Schoenberg's music and personality—Pitts Sanborn when he speaks of *Piérrot Lunaire's* kinship with El Greco, and Nicolas Slonimsky when he finds scriptural pathos in Schoenberg's epopeia:

"There is something biblical in Schoenberg's spectacular martyrdom. Shuttling between Vienna and Berlin, revered by disciples, derided by scurrilous critics, he is the very picture of a prophet of the faith. . . . Much has been said and written about Schoenberg's presentiment of a personal and general catastrophe, as evidenced by his paintings, his writings and his music. Subsequent events must have strengthened this morbid faith." [3]

* * *

The other edge of Jewish intellectual armour is even more harmful to the inborn, the best Hebrew creative self than an over-apostleship in murky tonal cults, a fervor sharpened by neurotic over-emphasis.

Interminable treading of the great cemetery of history by the Hebrew race, its worship in culture-asylums of all lands and all ages, has resulted in an inheritance even more calamitous than reflected thought and monstrous, humiliating flexibility.

Of the tonal offal picked up by the Jewish people

[3] Nicolas Slonimsky: *The Incoming Modern Master.* (Boston Transcript, October 1933).

along historic highways the worst is not the melodic
Oriental cliché, nor the pasticcio shaped after second-
rate regional styles, nor even the doctrinal speculation
and fanaticism of today's red musical wing. The worst
is that calamitous mission-idea that has made the Jewish
creator blind to his own submerged racial art. Blind
to the noble duty and to the exhilarating vista that
stretches before a son of the People of the Book. Eager
to take up a fantastic and fatal obligation to humanity,
that of an international musical salesman; eager to be
a citizen of the cosmopolitan art-realm. Anxious to
foster an insipid and cyclopean democratism of style like
Mahler of the symphonies. Eager to plant anarchical
individualism coupled with an all-cure tonal synthesis
like Schoenberg and Hauer, or to uphold the facile precepts of the "Latin genius" like Milhaud.

It is not messianism, but missionism that destroys
Jewish music now, just as classical pasticcio did formerly.

However, the channels of the race are *"aere perenius,"*
stronger than bronze. Authentic flames of Jewish tonal
genius do not turn their glow toward cosmopolitan missionary routes. *Spiritus movet ubi vult.* "The spirit
flows where it chooses." I speak of the cheering waves
of Bloch's *Israel,* Milner's beautiful Hebraic songs,
Achron's *Adon Olam,* Gniéssin's *Tomb of Rachel,*
Krein's *Ghazelen.*

THE JEWISHNESS OF WAGNER

Early in the sixteenth century a Spanish priest, Cardinal Don Francisco Mendoza y Bovadilla, wrote a book of considerable color and gusto, named *El tizon de la nobleza espagnola*. This book discusses the purity of blood of the Spanish aristocracy. Among other things he tells us, with pious indignation not unmixed with malice and hilarity, how one of the *nuevos christianos* (new Christians) managed to penetrate into the Spanish aristocracy and to marry off a flock of nine daughters to the most illustrious grandees of Spain, among them various royal dukes. In this way nefarious Jewish blood had contaminated even the royal tree of Castile and Aragon.

In excavating the roots of illustrious but doubtful Christians, all stories concerning veiled renegades invariably sound a malevolent delight. It is, perhaps, a gleam of contentment in historic justice that things will now be set aright.

* * *

The immortal controversy as to whether or not Wagner's paternity shows Jewish blood would never have acquired any particular weight, were he not a man of such magnitude, or more correctly, a composer of such magnitude; also, were he not the standard-bearer of a vicious antisemitic art-doctrine.

This is an extraordinary performance! A great composer of Jewish descent has willingly humiliated his own race! Has coined the ugly dictum that in *our* art *"Kann der Jude nur nachsprechen, nachkünsteln, nicht wirklich redend dichten, oder Kuntswerke shaffen"*— "the Jew can only mimic, imitate, not really speak his own, or create works of art!" [1] This disquiets the non-Jewish mind as well.

The sole way to untie the riddle and to relieve oneself from that blend of disgust and anxiety which this Wagner affair leaves in one, is to attack its first detail, Wagner's birth. If, after all, there is no trace of Jewish paternity in him, then his ideology is the natural aversion of a precious and pure-blooded Aryan for an exotic alien race.

Ernest Newman, distinguished critic, the highest authority on Wagner and the most detached and thorough investigator of Wagner's life, has this to say:

"On his father's side, the parentage of Richard Wagner is still a matter of dubiety." [2]

The eminent American musician Carl Engel has his subtle, humorous quips over Newman's *post mortem,* but, as I understand it, he evidently considers the illegitimacy of Wagner established.[3]

The details of Wagner's life, the significant hints in his intime dicta, letters exchanged with his sister cross- and con-examined by Newman so lucidly, point to a

[1] Richard Wagner: *Das Judenthum in der Musik,* in the third volume of Wagner's literary works.

[2] Ernest Newman: *The Life of Richard Wagner.* Alfred A. Knopf, New York 1933.

[3] Carl Engel: "Views and Reviews," *Musical Quarterly,* April 1933.

strong possibility that Richard Wagner's real father was the actor, Ludwig Geyer, a man of Jewish blood and a passionately devoted friend of the family long before he married Johanna Wagner.

"Wagner himself believed in the *possibility* of Geyer's having been his father," Newman thus underlines the result of his research.

One cannot refrain from pointing to Wagner's physical resemblance to Geyer, to his passion for all things theatrical, to many Jewish traits in both physique and character, such as a keen Oriental love of scents and colors, a curious blend of over-developed self-pity and repentance, etc.   Newman puts it very humorously: "Wagner enjoyed the luxury of repentance."   This is a typical Jewish enjoyment!   But no matter how strong all such circumstantial evidence may be, it is not half as potent as Wagner's own belief in Geyer having been his father.   In my opinion, this belief is conclusive, as far as Wagner's Jewish descent is concerned.

Taking it all in all, Wagner seems to have narrowly escaped the honor of a chapter in Gdal Saleski's well-known *Famous Musicians of a Wandering Race.*

*   *   *

Now, if the Jewishness of Wagner is an important issue, shall we revert to considering the torture of the renegade, to the obsession that follows even a part-Jewish psyche?

The distinguished Russian Hebrew composer, Michael Gniéssin, insists that it is not at all important whether or not Wagner was Jewish, that meaning lies only in a symbolic aspect of the story.   The name of a great musician who was also an imposing antisemite, is intertwined with a legend of his Jewish descent.

Even if Wagner was not a Jew who consciously belittled the spiritual stature of his race to dissociate himself from the Jews, there exist other Jew-Wagners who do so to rid themselves of the typical obsession of the renegade!

Gniéssin links this thought with an appraisal of the moods dominant among the Jewish composers of today.

Either brand is wrong:

those who scorn and repudiate their native art, revile the creative mind of their race, accuse it of intellectualism, formalism and lack of nature-sense;

or those who condition the salvage of Jewish music on the deserting of the cultural fields and ways of their neighbor.

Either trend has a sickly, a slave's viewpoint, one that underestimates and humiliates its own national force. The first of these complexes breeds an imaginary, above-depicted Jewish Wagner; the second expresses a reaction to the former psychology, a reaction dried into a shallow nationalist dogma.

To cramp Jewish creation and to stifle it by such ideology, is at best shortsighted, says Gniéssin. "We may be confident of the future of Jewish music. We can do as much as other nations. We must create freely and serenely, casting away the fear of being what we are."

* * *

Another well-known writer, Francis Toye of London, expresses just as forcefully, in his excellent book *The Well-tempered Musician,* his resistance to cultivated nationalism in music.

"A composer can no more flavor his music with nationalism to order than he may add a cubit to his stature...Nationalism is a kind of musical subconsciousness which may be instinctively called to the front, but never deliberately mobilized."

I will never agree with such a *laissez faire, laissez passer,* with this "let nature take its course." Even the safety valve of such a policy, Gniéssin's "overcoming of the fear of being what we are," does not in itself open the road to a full utilizing of the authentic Jewish tonal genius.

After all, what has Western culture gained from making Jewish art imitative? From the denaturing of a bright and original racial psyche, from causing it to lose its autonomous worth through centuries of foreign pressure? Does not every Jewish composer suffer from alien cultural loads that weigh down his native spirituality? Are we not possessed, cruelly so, of a sense of bondage in our creative effort; are we not tortured by a curtain between ourselves and our spiritual eye? Are we not pained by a yearning to rewin our true, elemental diction that still winters in our own racial soil?

Why, the urge of communion with the race even in an elementary way, such as the cultivating of the Jewish folksong, is in itself a repudiation of Gniéssin's *laissez faire, laissez passer.*

*　*　*

But cast aside these more complicated issues as to
Hebrew creation involved in our diatribe. I am still
not ready to abandon the clear import of our battle.
Wagner, both the Jew and the anti-Jew, is too firmly,
too meaningfully tied to a string of æsthetic and social
philosophies that poison the mind of the so-called civilized man of the West. One has no right to leave the
controversy as it now stands.

An unexplored avenue of access to Wagner's Jewishness exists, that of the Semitic or Oriental traits in his
creative self. Examine the whole spirit of his tonal and
dramatic conception. *Tristan* is, perhaps, the best field
for such inquiry.

It is illuminating to find in Wagner's *Tristan* no
sympathetic cord of a purely Aryan nature, no feeling
for the Celtic emotional medium. Neither does one
find here concrete life-detail and psychology native to
the *Europaische Mensch,* traits that distinctly pervade
the Arthurian legends. It seems that the great aggressive
Aryan Wagner had no flair for the elevated Celtic love-
sense, love-manner, nor for any other point of the old
Aryan code of chivalry. Wagner's eroticism is eminently
and bluntly Oriental. Out of numberless delicate detail
of the Celtic legends, his selection and his predilection
is but for episodes of high color and of primitive sexuality, a basis for choice that is fatally Oriental. In Wagner's sexuality there is more of the patriarchal Hebrew
"our seed and our progeny He will multiply like sand
on the sea-shore," than of the inexorable, tribal and
sex-shy restraint of the ancient Saxon, or the dimmed
symbolic troth of the ancient Celt.

It is quite illuminating that Wagner discarded the quaint episode of the second Isolda. This episode as found in the old Celtic legends, sets a clear contrast of the true Aryan or Celtic or Nordic love-sense with Wagner's exotic eroticism.

Exiled from the court of King Marc, Tristan is forced unwittingly by his friend, Prince Kahedin of Brittany, to marry his sister, another Isolda, *Iseut aux Blanches Mains,* that is, "Isolda of the White Hands." As the quaint old saga says, Tristan marries her *"pour son nom et pour sa beauté."* The marriage is not consummated, however; on the wedding night Tristan is conscious of the ring given him by the first Isolda, the one of Cornwales, and he repents of his marriage.[4]

In Sir Thomas Malory's *Le Morte D'Arthur* (The Death of King Arthur), that medieval amalgamation of the Celtic legends, Tristan writes to Lancelot that "as he was a true knight, he had never ado fleshly with Isoud le Blaunche Maynys."

Much as I would dislike a note of frivolity in this discussion, I cannot refrain from saying that Wagner's sexual imagination could not have conceived of this.

After copious digging into Celtic mythology, Wagner passed by this fine episode of the second Isolda, priceless dramatic material. That he did so, cannot be explained away as simply as exigencies of dramatic unity. Wagner did not exert himself about such niceties in his muddled librettos; it is enough to recall the *Nibelungen* jungle.

---

[4] See the book of the brilliant young Oxford savant and authority on Celtic lore, Dr. Eugene Vinaver: *Le roman de Tristan et Iseut dans l'œuvre de Thomas Malory.* Librarie Champion, Paris, 1925.

His omitting of the second Isolda altogether shows that he had no flair for the Aryan medieval love-vision, no feeling for the ethereal, almost religious fidelity of the *trouvère's* love-striving.   In this case as in others, Wagner, with an elemental and bluntly Eastern perception of sex, bares his dramatic scheme of all but naked and primitive erotic crises, and his color-scheme of all but brutal hues.

One is tempted to jest that *Tristan* is a Jewish treatment of a Celtic subject.

It is very amusing to see what an undiluted Aryan or a Celt has to say about *Tristan's* emotional outspokenness.   In a letter from Bayreuth, Vernon Lee writes to Maurice Baring:

"*Tristan* is indecent through its dragging out of situations, its bellowing out of confessions which the natural human being dreads to profane by showing or expressing." [5]

Just as *Tristan*, the rest of Wagner's music abounds in demonstration of what Wagner's tonal medium and its emotional and sexual tonus really are: very little "Aryan," rather over-expressive and exotic.   Sigmund's hysterical outcry, in the scene of Hunding's challenge—in *Die Walküre's* first act—"*Wälse, Wälse, wo ist dein Schwert, das starke Schwert,*"—this neurotic shriek, is it "Aryan"?   Why, it is more kindred to the possessed religious shout of a Galician synagogue than to the heart of Bach's or Handel's progeny.   It is much more germane to the synagogal "*Gegurgel, Gejodel, Geklapper*"

[5] Maurice Baring: *The Puppet Show of Memory*.   Little, Brown and Company, Boston 1922.

which Wagner talks of so cuttingly, than to Bach's *Aria* or the Adagio from Beethoven's fourth symphony.

It will be worth considering how lurid Wagner's own overemphasis and exoticism are when opposed to the rigid, cyclopean classicism of Mendelssohn, Rubinstein and other Jews in music. And these are supposed to have contaminated the Aryan-pure European art with their alien accent and flavor,—to listen to Wagner, Liszt, Stewart Houston Chamberlain and, indeed, to Gobineau, father of the *asemitic* creed.

* * *

I am far from being an enemy of the race-concept. I am a stubborn believer in the seminal might and in the cultural fertility that flow from the blood. But Heaven protect us from allies of the Gobineau and Chamberlain ilk!

Learning that uses an ax instead of the engraving needle or a medical scissors; science that gathers observation on most intricate race-complexes in pleasure-boats, on chance trips to the East; wisdom that builds syllogisms out of obsessions and nightmares, is truly comical. There is much of a sergeant-major turned professor in such "Aryan" savants.

The basis for Wagner's and Chamberlain's denunciation of the Jewish poison is the incredible, quasi-learned vinaigrette in four volumes named *Sur l'inégalité des races humaines* [6] of that queer graphomaniac, Count Artur de Gobineau. His disciple, the renegade son-in-law of Wagner, Steward Houston Chamberlain, is just as

6 Published by Firmin Diderot Frères, Paris 1853.

flimsy in his quasi-savant documentation and just as fantastic in his broad assertions as is Gobineau.

Chamberlain is the man who said that Heine is a microscopic poet deprived of any lyric sense. He insists, in his book *Rasse und Persönlichkeit,* that in spite of a complete assimilation of language and habits of the land, the Langobards, that Teutonic barbarian race which conquered Lombardy in the sixth century C.E., were still absolutely pure racially as late as in the fifteenth century. He believes Dante to be *"ein Germane reinster Abkunft."* This is the gentleman who said of the Jews: *"Als Gesamterscheinung bedeuten die Juden ein unleugbare grosze Gefahr fur unsere Kultur; hier addieren sich die bedenklichen Charakterzüge und neutralisieren sich die annerkennens-werten."* [7]

Men of such mental levity, irresponsible, loose in handling scientific facts, have fed Wagner's and Liszt's *asemitic* wisdom.

It is amusing to see their Aryan indictment dwindle down to two points diametrically opposed.

First, the Jewish musical jargon is ultra-expressive and ultra-exotic spiritual mud; it hides no creative potency whatsoever, and it is entirely opposed to Aryan tonal thought.

Second, the Jewish intonation and expressiveness filter insidiously into the pure medium of Aryan thought; defiles and degenerates it.

[7] "As a collective phenomenon the Jews mean an unmistakably great danger to our culture; because of them preposterous traits are added (to our culture) and those worthy of recognition and preservation are being neutralized." Stewart Houston Chamberlain: *Die Rasse und Persönlichkeit.* F. Bruckman, Munich 1925.

In his famous speech on the casuistics through which Jewish members of the British Parliament were barred for generations from taking their lawful seats in the House of Commons, Thomas Macaulay shows with delicious clarity how the same reasoning is applied in favor of the Catholic and against the Jewish emancipation:

"When the question was about Catholic emancipation, the cry was: 'See how restless, how versatile, how encroaching, how insinuating, is the spirit of the Church of Rome. See how her priests compass earth and sea to make one proselyte, how indefatigably they toil, how skillfully they employ literature, arts and sciences, as engines for the propagation of their faith. . . . Will you give power to the members of a Church, so busy, so aggressive, so insatiable?' Well, now the question is about people who never try to seduce any stranger to join them, and who do not wish anybody to be of their faith, who is not also of their blood, the Jews. And now you exclaim, 'Will you give power to the members of a sect which remains sullenly apart from other sects, which does not invite, nay, which hardly even admits, neophytes?' The truth is, bigotry will never want a pretence." [8]

The case is laughably the same as with the Aryan dogma of Chamberlain-Wagner.

On one side, the Aryan racial protoplasm is so strong that it took the Langobards ten centuries to dilute it in the Italian sea; on the other, the weak and muddy

---

[8] Lord Macaulay, Baron of Rothley: *Jewish Disabilities*, speech delivered in the House of Commons on April 17, 1833. See Macaulay's Complete Works, Volume VIII. Longmans, Green and Co., London 1866.

Jewish thought, of no creative power whatsoever, is a horrible menace to the purity of Aryan craft.

In fine, it is the formula that rules the courtesies between the lady on the Niger and her friend, the tiger: "Your argument is flawless yet insignificant in face of the fact that I am going to devour you." An attitude which is useless to fight with anything but the bludgeon. Better still to merely pass it by.

*　　*　　*

However, if it is well to forgo the pitiable philosophies of a Gobineau or a Chamberlain, it will not do to pass by lightly vituperations fostered by men and minds of Wagner's and Liszt's stature.

There exists that bulky book on music of the Hungarian gypsies by Liszt, a veritable waterfall of verbiage that circumnavigates in high fever every topic but gypsy music. Liszt admits the Jewish musicians to be useful, even indispensable, agents of musical progress, but he, too, insists that the Jews do not possess true creative ability. His formula is subtler and more diplomatic, or more *decent* than those of Wagner and Chamberlain. One does expect this from a generous, a grand nature such as Liszt's.

But the venom is there. *"Les Juifs ne se permettent pas autre chose que d'agencer, de combiner, de marrier les éléments que nous créons."*—"The Jews do not allow themselves anything else but to trim, to combine and to marry the elements which we create." [9]

And he follows this up with a flock of veiled or frank

[9] Franz Liszt: *Des Bohémiens et de leur musique en Hongrie.* Breitkopf und Haertel, Leipzig 1881.

innuendoes, good-natured or poisoned laudations of Jewish propaganda. He points to the over-excitement and musical expansion created by the Jews in the performing sphere; he subtly slanders the exotic nature of their success on the concert platform, their gift for using artistic supremacy for social advancement.

That Liszt should lament it! The Great Gypsy himself, father of all things exotic in European music for nearly a century, progenitor of over-emphasis and the drawing-room perfumery that mark the new interpretive avenues! The creator of new methods of sensation that would put the musician in bolder relief! Liszt, of all people, is vexed by Jewish over-excitement, over-expressiveness and what not!

One cannot refrain from opposing to Liszt's innuendoes the poised and scrupulously honest judgment of a man of our own day, Dr. Goldberg's appraisal of the lowliest product of Jewish creation:

"Into the business (of Tin Pan Alley) the Jew could no more help bringing something of the racial poetry than could the Negro and the Irishman. A humble poetry, a lowly conception of words and music, yet tinged indelibly with the hue of folk-feeling and folk-thought.[10]

* * *

Accusations against the Jewish exotic platform-manner still live, a hang-over of that vicious smoke of the Wagner-Chamberlain blessings.

[10] Dr. Isaac Goldberg: *Tin Pan Alley*. John Day Company, New York 1930.

I remember the appearance, during the war, of a
remarkable book, *Modernism and Music,* by a well-
known Russian-German writer and adherent of the
asemitic doctrine who had chosen as a *nom de plume*
the name of Wolfing. This serious philosophical book
changes its tone at once as soon as it approaches the Jewish musician. Then we find elegant sentences, tempered
with a true Nordic restraint:

"All these Ossips, Grishas and Mishas resemble one
another like one decent violin resembles the next one.
They all play with the same assurance; exhibit ostentatiously their none too clean technic; behave with the
same arrogance on the platform. The cleverest vaguely
suspicious of the public's love for everything 'exotic'
give themselves a ferocious look in highly dynamic
passages or a 'romantic' expression in a cantilena while
trying to spice the latter with the nauseating Southern
sweetened passion which disrupts the European style in
a most inartistic, barbarian way."

It is curious that these lines were written just at the
time of Jascha Heifetz's first triumphs, when everyone
was carried away by the sacramental purity, by a Hel-
lenic spirituality and detachment in this wonder-boy's
playing and also by his uncommonly beautiful, somewhat somber and stern, princely appearance.

The eminent Moscow musician and critic and a snow-
white Nordic to boot, Leonide Sabanéyev, ministered a
strong and just rebuke to Herr Wolfing's too colorful
tableau. "Let us recall that all those violin and zimbalon
players, Rumanians, Hungarians, Gypsies, those men

primitively exotic, dark-eyed, passionate in an inferior way, are 'Aryans'. If one is to compare the exoticism of a Kubelik or a Stefanesco with that of a Rubinstein or a Joachim, there is not the slightest doubt as to who will be the winner." [11]

Of course, it is only normal for the Jewish people to possess *their* merchants in music. Other nations have them in various well-known creative and interpretive artists with no Jewish blood in their veins.

In the complex problems of Hebrew art-psychology should one, however, take seriously the opinion of writers who judge the spiritual caliber of a Jewish performer not by a Mahler, a Joachim, a Rubinstein, a Heifetz, a Godowski, a Gabrilovitch, a Szigetti, a Horowitz or a Menuhin, but by manufactured wares, by the Grishas and Mishas of the Berlin or New York concert-platform? All of these artists dwell on the same spiritual heights as Toscanini, Furthwängler, Busoni or any other of the great non-Jewish musicians.

Together with Wagner, Wolfing hears in the old synagogal music, that realm of the loftiest folk-art, nothing but *"Gegurgel, Gejodel, Geklapper"*. Were Herr Wolfing to deal with the music of Dagomeans, Andaman islanders or the savages of Patagonia, he would find himself bound to know his subject better and treat it more deferentially. But he speaks only of the People of the Book, and any "Aryan" jest is a good enough *specimen eruditionis*.

* * *

11 Leonide Sabanéyev: *Music and Patriotism* in No. 107 of the magazine "Music," Moscow.

But let us return to our main road and ask what really is repellent in Wagner's *bavardage* concerning Jewishness in music? Why does a faint odor of the unreal hover about these *asemitic* dissertations? What is the root of their disability?

The most disagreeable and the most puzzling thing about the discussion, also the source of a peculiar poignancy and mistrust that it provokes, is not the doctrine in itself. The latter is too clearly a civilized garment for racial antipathy.

Our disgust of this caddish side of Wagner's epopeia comes from an inner confession that it is just because this man was more likely than not of Jewish blood and hated it, that he felt the urge of making racial antipathy into a dogma that belittles and reviles the spiritual physiognomy of the Hebrew race. True "Aryans", or men of Hindu-German race, true *Europaische Menschen* such as Beethoven or Schubert, Debussy or Rimski-Korsakov, did not notice the Jewish menace. The shadow of the Jew in music did not disturb them at all.

HEBREW AMERICAN COMPOSERS

This colorful and active phalanx breaks up into several distinct sections. The cleavage is only too natural in the case of a group bristling with complexities, tangles and incongruities of a highly mixed creative psychology.

The first and foremost division, foremost in renown, mastery and influence, includes Ernest Bloch and Louis Gruenberg.[1]

They crystallized at once and leave no doubt as to their scope and stature. One knew what to expect from them at the very outset. Of the two, Bloch has more oneness and more evenness in his æsthetic planning. He is a master of clarity and poised might which now and then stoops to a Jewish bourgeois self-content. And this in spite of a certain Job-like capacity for lament and self-pity.

Gruenberg is multichrome, sumptuous and verbose. He is less definite and less directly Jewish than Bloch. But his speech is stamped by a greater exquisiteness of choice and a restlessness, and his mastery by greater in-

[1] In her foreword to *American Composers*, the excellently compiled record of American works issued by the American Section of the International Society for Contemporary Music, Claire Reis points to the many ingredients of the melting pot of American music: the English ballad, the cowboy song, the Indian melody and Negro jazz, of course. Mrs. Reis would be fully justified in adding the important neo-Hebraic element which reveals itself in the American Northeast.

quest. Here he has the supremacy over Bloch who is not loath to employ the facile, the *trouvaille* found on the walks of a too easy artistry. In the novelty of tempo, in his blunt demolition of hide-bound musical habits, Gruenberg towers over the entire progressive wing of the American composers of today, somewhat over-crowded with scantly taught musicians and with radical reformers of things they never knew.

One admires Gruenberg's scrupulous musicianship and lordly hold of tone-color in the *Jazz-suite;* the elegant and subtle culture of his tonal thinking in the *Jazz-berries;* his verve and bolts of gargantuan gayety in the irresistible finale of *Daniel Jazz.* And yet, one feels a pathetic rift within his creation. Something with an upset creative stem.

This is an odd picture. A son of Israel and a grandson of Isaiah, marked with all their emotional loftiness, their moral directness, their torrential and keen loquac-ity, forces his creation through the channel of Black Melos!

Why should a Gruenberg, who has every requisite of a Hebrew creator and who could have become a shining banner-bearer of Hebrew art, why should *he* turn mouthpiece of the Negro, his soul, its prank and pain?

Have there not been enough queer rôles already played by Jewish creative musicians, without adding to a picture of camouflage and confusion still another odd exhibit?

Let us have it out once forever. In the summit of Gruenberg's production, in his opera *Emperor Jones,* I do not object so much to its æsthetic and operatic shortcomings, as I deplore an immense lugubrious travail misdirected and misspent.

In fact, I consider *Emperor Jones* an important event of operatic history. I do not subscribe to the opinion that *Emperor Jones* is not an opera, but incidental music to a drama. Even less would I endorse the verdict that the music has added nothing to O'Neill's drama, to its unique drive and theatrical brilliancy.

Let us dispense with the notion that the mere discarding of set vocal forms, of arias and choruses of the old stamp, disintegrates a musical drama's operatic nature. Like Alban Berg's *Wozzeck,* and other new musical dramas that have introduced the speaking-singing voice (*die Sprechstimme*) as a major vocal-dramatic medium, Louis Gruenberg's *Emperor Jones* has simply taken the second step in the liberation of the opera from the yoke of set instrumental forms. The first step was Wagner's transfer of a great deal of the dramatic and descriptive functions from the human voice, center of the old opera, to its orchestral and symphonic organ.

The spoken word of Gruenberg's *Emperor Jones* is, as a rule, very different from O'Neill's spoken word. Gruenberg's *Sprechstimme* and recitative have their own tonal curve and pitch. They are subordinated to, and governed by, a very different tonal logic: that of musical expression, of musical form and musical description. This fact in itself lends special value to Gruenberg's musical counterpart of O'Neill's drama.

Without the additional drive and menace contained in Gruenberg's tonal scenery, the last scene of the opera —where Jones, cornered by the savage crowd of bush

Negroes, shoots himself—would never attain that tense pitch of human agony, of limitless elemental poignancy, which render the scene so convincing and operatically so true.

But after all is said, what of it? Gruenberg's mental and emotional pitch, his sure mastery and high technical culture could achieve the extraordinary were they applied to the woof of the *Golem* legend,[2] for instance, or to a dramatic tale of the Spanish Jewry's martyrdom under the Inquisition, or to one of those smiling, lovable chassidic stories of Peretz, the great Polish Jewish writer of the nineteenth century. But the felicity of living in communion with the lore and the emotion of one's own race is not granted to Gruenberg. This has cost him dearly as it has others.

*   *   *

Schopenhauer says somewhere that to a Frenchman or an Englishman a mentioned "idea" will carry a very definite, a well circumscribed meaning: but suggest one to a German, and he acts as if he were soaring in a balloon. Such is the familiar reaction of even the mediocre Jewish artist or savant as soon as he takes the pose of seership. Jewish thought seems to be condemned to flounder in a superman's exaggeration.

In his admirable *Aspects of Rabbinic Theology*, Dr. Solomon Schechter, the great leader of Orthodox Judaism in America, strikes at these hyperboles efficiently.

---

[2] Golem the evildoer, was a gigantic statue built of clay and given life by the famous rabbi and miracle-maker, Yehudah Löw of Prague (sixteenth century). Finally the rabbi found it necessary to destroy the *Golem* who brought ruin to the Prague ghetto.

"I have often marvelled at the certainty and confidence with which Jewish legalism, Jewish transcendentalism, Jewish self-righteousness, are delineated in our theological manuals and histories of religion. . . . But I have never been able to emulate either quality." [3]

This innate Jewish pose, dogmatic and prophetic at the same time, is the source of Ernest Bloch's forceful platitudes, musical or otherwise. But I wish to immediately qualify this statement by pointing out that by their very origin, these trite pronunciamentos are traditional rather than personal.

It is true that Bloch's own predilection for donning the hood of a Hebrew prophet, and Bloch's declarations, old and new, that his music "is addressed to all mankind," has let loose much sumptuous over-statement.

Paul Rosenfeld, I believe, is one of those who tempted the flood.

"The voice of Jehovah, has it spoken to those who throughout the ages called for it much differently than it speaks at the close of Bloch's XXII Psalm?" [4]

The old story of the apostles explaining the prophet to himself to his complete transfiguration! Sabanéyev transforming Scriabin into a mystagogue, Schloezer making an "objective" composer of Stravinski, and Rosenfeld presenting Bloch with the passport of Isaiah. Even Leigh Henry, who has said many lucid things concerning Bloch, calls him "the Isaiah of modern music

---

[3] Dr. Solomon Schechter: *Some Aspects of Rabbinic Theology*. Macmillan Co., New York 1909.

[4] Paul Rosenfeld: *Musical Portraits*. Harcourt, Brace and Howe, New York 1920.

par excellence", attributes to him "the broad epic vision of the seer." [5]

One should discard his artificial messianic light; then only is the absolute, the personal depth of Ernest Bloch probed, his real worth assayed. I would say that, as in Mahler's case, Bloch's pose as the Almighty's lieutenant denatures or even submerges his best traits. Nothing does one wish so much as to forget the "marmoreal greatness" of Ernest Bloch and to come closer to his lovable, human and lyric self; to listen to him when his speech is free from spiritual stilts, in the *Quintet* or in "How lovely are thy tents, O Jacob" from the *Sacred Service*. Still, Bloch's grand inflation, assumed and facile, is overshadowed by a unicolored formal oneness. This flows as much from his native and unsplit racial direction as it does from his clear artistry and robust mental trunk.

Roger Sessions, the well-known composer and leader of the younger American group, has said very justly indeed, that Bloch "quite consciously reveals an ideal self, rather than an actual one." [6]

Here is the key to Bloch's complexities, to his weal and woe.

His ideal self which he stubbornly fosters in conformity with a somewhat shallow, quasi-traditional mold, lands him in no end of Hebraistic platitude which gains nothing from being ultra-categoric or violent. This is where we find the sickly, ghetto-ridden echo,

---

[5] Leigh Henry: "Two Hebrew Composers," in the *Musical Standard*, London, 1925.

[6] Roger Sessions: "Ernest Bloch," *Modern Music*, 1927.

such as the crawling and whining, quasi-Ecclesiastean and pseudo-Jewish first theme of *Shelomo,* the quasi-mystic melopeia of *Adon Olam* in the *Sacred Service,* the banal, penny-Judaism of the *Baal-Shem* suite.

But Bloch's actual self, his personal and mighty emotion when flaming in true rhythm with his race without taking the visionary stand, is responsible for glowing pages that will remain in time's memory.   The opening of *Israel,* the fulgent *coda* from *Shelomo,* the telling serenity of *Ma towu* (How lovely are thy tents, O Jacob) in the *Sacred Service,* here is actual triumph for the new musical art of Israel!   One readily agrees with clear characterization of Bloch's *Psalm cxxxvii* by the distinguished Italian writer, Guido Gatti: "Its asymmetries, its angulosities, its barbaric simplicities, even its insufficient variety of harmonic combinations, all aid in matching the power of the biblical narrative." [7]

*   *   *

Another Hebrew American group also draws its distinction from a typical but a rather new racial color. It is composed of musicians whose tonal mind is clearly traceable even when their creative level can not be gauged with assurance.   Leo Ornstein, Aaron Copland and George Gershwin, of whom I speak, constitute the decidedly Yiddish constellation among the composers of this country.   There is not a drop of the Hebraic in their music, not a cell of the blood of Jacob.   This music abounds in ghetto *raffinement* or regeneration,

[7] Guido M. Gatti: "Ernest Bloch," *Musical Quarterly,* New York. 1921.

whatever you may call it.   It abounds in a rampant
Judaic breath (Judaic as opposed to Hebraic).   Scriabin
was able to alter Ornstein as little as Mahler *plus* jazz
to galvanize Copland, or Rimski-Korsakov *plus* the
Broadway folksong, to disarray the native substance of
Gershwin.

Paul Rosenfeld has seized on Ornstein's Yiddish
nucleus very accurately:

> "The Jewish spirit come up into the day from
> out the basement and cellar rooms of the synagogue
> where it had been seated for a thousand years drug-
> ging itself with rabbinical lore, refining almost
> maniacally upon the intention of some obscure
> phrase or parable, negating the lure of the world." [8]

At times, however, arresting lines of grandeur gleam
through the medium of Ornstein's melancholy and
wordy and facile Judaic melos.   These rise from a moral
elevation also born in the throes of the ghetto; born in
its fortitude and grandiose philosophies that are to
alleviate the ghastly week-day of bondage.   In this light
the strange clinging of Ornstein to the elevated, mystic
lines of Scriabin's tonal cosmology is, perhaps, not so
difficult to explain.

In a certain sense, Gershwin has significance that is
not granted to other Americans.   He was part of the
jazz-feast that managed in its short day to shake the very
girders of our comfortable musical structure out of its
lazy joints.   His personal share in this useful entertainment was the transmuting of the rude animal din of

[8] Paul Rosenfeld in *Musical Portraits*.

Negro jazz into real music, human and elegant, full of enchanting tonal subtleties.

Some of the most fastidious and the distinguished among American writers on art have marked the broader promise hidden in Gershwin's work or, at least, the personal breeze in his intuition.

Lawrence Gilman, usually an unrelenting censor of the Gershwin art, could not help admitting, in a fascinating dictum, "its gusto and naïveté, its tang of a new and urgent world, engaging, ardent, unpredictable."

Reappraising the general import of Gershwin and his share in the jazz-attainments, another writer of eminence, Dr. Isaac Goldberg, says of jazz, with his admirable fairness and precision:

> "It is greeted with self-protective hostility; it is traceable in part to the Negro; it is developed, commercially and artistically by the Jew . . . to academic timorousness is added social prejudice . . . a symptom of rebellion against routine—not only the pitiless routine of living, but the sterilized routine of musical academism. . . .
> . . . To jazz, accused of being only animal excitement, Gershwin has brought a strong suggestion of what, for lack of a better term, we call spiritual values. Slowly, to these dimensions, he is adding depth.". . .[9]

Let us, however, leave generalities concerning Gershwin and dwell for a time on the Jewish or rather Yiddish dialect of his music.

Gershwin himself confessed to me: "While I actually

[9] Dr. Isaac Goldberg: *George Gershwin*. Simon and Schuster, New York 1931.

do not know much about Jewish folksong, I think that many of my themes are Jewish in feeling although they are purely American in style." This statement is remarkably correct from either of its angles.

The idea that the Gershwin themes are Negroid, with the rest of the "jazzberries", is a sorry knot of inaccuracies. The popular American Negro song is not African, but eminently American and notably Anglo-Celtic. It has not travelled as far as from the lake of Tchad or Victoria-Nyanza, but arrived, an unpretentious tourist, from the shores of Loch Lomond or Killarney. The melodic turn and cadence of such famous Negro spirituals as *Deep River* or *Nobody Knows the Trouble I Am In,* are Scotch and Irish cadences typical of our Southern and American mountaineer song. The American child has not adapted the songs of the Negro mammy; it was the mammy who grew bewitched by the Celtic-American ditty. But the warm Negro instinct has added to the Anglo-Celtic tune a rhythmic twist and emotional glow, in fine, some "southern exultation".

His instinct, then, does not deceive Gershwin when he insists that the style of his themes is American, in a direct sense. He is equally right as to their Jewish feeling. But his tonal Jewishness is of a highly spiced flavor.

The *Rhapsody in Blue* opens with a typical Yiddish-Roumanian soliloquy—a sort of a Roumanian *doyna:* the clarinet solo. It has the gait and the hue of a Balkan-Jewish wedding tune, is personalized in an attractive manner and encased in a subtle and fresh harmonic frame. But the tonal air is contaminated by a strange blend of odors; distant smoke from Rimski-Korsakov's *Spanish Capriccio,* Liszt's *Hungarian Rhapsodies,* Mississippi *Blues* and what not.

There is a peculiar glow and glamour in the climactic passages of the *Rhapsody in Blue.* Its closing segment reflects the duality of a mixed tonal idiom: one is impressed by both, a verve and lilt lent by the American or the Anglo-Celtic popular song and by the traces of a distinct Jewish exultation.

As to the *Concerto in F,* in its more fastidious first theme one senses a subtle and attractive *Yiddishism.* Something which might adorn the mystic dreams of the young *Talmudist*-student from the *Dibbuk*-legend.[10] But again, the flat exotic undervoice of the *Spanish Capriccio* debases what could be elevated to a personal style.

*   *   *

A gifted American, Theodore Chanler, quotes: "Someone has said that Aaron Copland's musical ideas are like pennies shrewdly invested rather than pearls advantageously set." [11]

I dislike to generalize in the cruel pinning down of Copland's value. But his work, a mature one, his trio *Vitebsk* (Study on a Jewish melody) seems to embody an artisanship that smacks of "penny-investing", and not an especially shrewd gamble either.

Let no one say that this is a chance work, a passing

10 *Dibbuk* is the soul of a sinner which, after his death, enters the body of someone the sinner was in love with.

11 *American Composers on American Music,* a symposium edited by Henry Cowell, Stanford University Press, 1933.

improvisation drawn up in a moment of affection for a lovely Jewish melody. A Copland work is a scheme rather than a composition. It is usually a highly pains-taking and protracted venture. He sometimes spends years in weaving one single small work. He does not trust his intuition and composes neither swiftly nor spontaneously.

All the Copland calculation is there, even in the sub-title "a study", a sort of insurance against criticism. But even this safety device does not ward off or mitigate the impression of an insipid, petty and unimaginative treat-ment of a fine Jewish folksong.

The texture of the *Trio* is an obvious and naïve hash: cheap polytonal spices, atonal ornament, lame canons and disjointed imitation dragged from keyboard base-ment to the fiddling heights. The well-known arsenal of the nurseries of modernity!

The fine folk-chantey used is a typical episode, an exotic refrain, rather than a theme. To apply to it the drab machinery of thematic development, elementary preparation of theme-entrances *à la* Tschaikovski (prep-aration of the second section *Allegro vivace,* for example) and other Western-academic proceedings, re-veals a lack of vision, a blindness to the wonderful possibilities hidden in this enchanting refrain.

Byron said that every detail of Beau Brummell's dress had an exquisite propriety about it. Copland's *Trio* is singular in a repulsive impropriety of garb. Its Jewish-ness is musically shallow, and its motives opportunistic. After the subtle, poised and finished mastery achieved by Bloch, Achron and Gniéssin, in their treatment of

Hebrew melos, this *Study on a Jewish Melody* sounds like sheer effrontery.

One is tempted to paraphrase the tart word of a dissatisfied Venetian courtesan to Jean-Jacques Rousseau which he quotes in his *Confessions*:

"Zanetto, lascia le donne e studia la matamatica"— "Little Jean, drop the ladies and study mathematics." [12] "Mathematics"—in this case the planting of jazzberries —were, perhaps, better for Copland, too.   He touches Jewish melos furtively.   His is a back-door sort of communion; he does not wish, or is not able, to consecrate himself in earnest, deep submergence in the song of his race.   He should leave it and return to the pranks of polytonal jazz.

And yet, the rôle of a master in jazz sublimation is not Copland's own, either.   He has tried to wrest the coronet from Gershwin.   But lovely Jazzerella—to evoke Lawrence Gilman's delicious silhouette—who embraces Gershwin with such affection, has treated Copland to only a few fascinating jilts in his *Concerto* and vanished.

Stylization of the jazz-pattern, the condensing of the jazz-spirit into a cultured form, and even the peculiar neurotic exhilaration of jazz, is not native to Copland; that is clear now.   His interest was a policy, a temporary pose greedily taken during the jazz storm of the Hilarious Twenties.   It is a relief to know that the unsavoury, shrieking cartwheels from *Music for the Theatre* is the artificial, the casual Copland.   That the wistful, earnest and delicate slow melos of this piece is the best and the Jewish Copland.   That this sombre melopeia reflects

12 Jean Jacques Rousseau: *Confessions*, Livre VII.

the something stately and still and subtle which is the charm of Copland the man.

In this scrambled world one owes much, compellingly so, to truth. That wrong sort of politeness, dubbed so excellently by Samuel Johnson "fictitious benevolence", has filled the scrolls of appraisal with flaccid false praise of the pseudo-progressive. I am sorry to profess an eradicable conviction that Copland is of an observing, an absorbing nature, rather than a creative one. In this he is a sort of miniature Mahler; this kinship in mentality is perhaps the reason for Copland's Mahler-worship.

*   *   *

I now come to an American group that bears perhaps the faintest Hebrew mark; it seems, moreover, rather heterogeneous as to mental type and artistry.

Yet there is something very definitely in common in these three composers: Frederick Jacobi, Bernard Rogers and Israel Citkowitz. They all belong to the Mendelssohnian type of Hebrew creative musicianship; they share in some measure in its worship of culture, in its earnest and gentle workmanship. With the *Sabbath Evening Service,* his most mature and his unmistakably personal work,[13] Frederick Jacobi has undergone a striking change, both technical and creative. If the "Adoration", the *Va'anachnu koreim,* of this service is the loftiest bit of music ever written by Jacobi, his *V'shomru b'ne Israel* is the warmest, the most colorful and true,

---

[13] Frederick Jacobi: *Sabbath Evening Service* for cantor, chorus and organ, sponsored by the Choir Committee of Congregation Emanu-El, New York (Bloch Publishing Company).

more so even than his attractive *String Quartet* built on Indian themes.

Jacobi's *Concerto* for cello and orchestra has inherited some Hebraic marks from the *Service*. The opening theme with its *Mixolydian* turn has the kindly serenity of a Hebrew *Ma tovu*. But the work as a whole is less vital, less outspoken in its Hebraic pathos than the *Service,* a distinctive contribution to the new American music.

In Bernard Rogers' early orchestral poem, *To the Faithful,* as well as in his later *Adonais*-symphony and *Second String Quartet,* a lyric directness is, perhaps, the most appealing quality. However, after the melancholy grace of these works, the exuberance of Rogers' latest oratorio *The Exodus* and its virile biblical stamp are very refreshing.

In speaking of Bernard Rogers and his rôle in the American Hebrew *musicalia,* one must note a group of his highly gifted Jewish disciples whom he has taught, jointly with the eminent American composer and educator, Dr. Howard Hanson, at the Eastman Conservatory in Rochester. Among them I would mention Irving Landau, author of the remarkably forceful and mature *Variations* for orchestra, and David Diamond, composer of the delicately somber *Hebrew Songs* and *Ashen Pages* for voice and orchestra. Together with the phalanx of outstanding young New Yorkers, grouping mainly around Henry Cowell, such as Henry Brant, Evelyn Berckman, Jerome Moross, Miriam Gideon and Vivian Fine, they form the constellation of the promising younger Hebrew American talent.

The most impressive traits of Israel Citkowitz's works, of his string quartet and the delectable songs, are the elegance of tonal thought and the neat culture and deftness of his technical manner.   It is a relief to find a Citkowitz figure, a poised and tenacious intelligence, in the hectic parliament of half-baked and over-publicized young gentlemen, who form the ever ready supply for the "radical" coteries of New York and points West.

But one member of the younger Hebrew American group stands out, not only in his brilliant musicianship and unusualness of creative and critical mind, but also, in the peculiarity of his position.   This is Marc Blitzstein.

There is a kinship with Schoenberg in Blitzstein's tortured and aloof concept; something cruel and intentionally arid, reminding one of Schoenberg's *Woodwind Quintet*.   The structural and aesthetic logic is wise and lucid, the human and emotional logic queer, incomprehensible.   Blitzstein's opera *Caïn,* his most direct and forceful work, holds out an aesthetic and human promise which clearly forbids our judgment any measure of finality.

A RUSSIAN JEWISH GROUP

In a line with Ernest Bloch, four masters holding Russian Jewish musical hegemony, Michel Gniéssin, Moses Milner, Joseph Achron and Alexander Krein, represent the true musical Israel of today; they are its best or even its only real voice.

Gniéssin, a cloistered mentality of strong distinction, should be considered this group's leader; Milner, its genius and its Dionysius; Achron, standard-bearer of its neo-Hebraic craft, and Krein, seeker after its new Hebrew diction.

*   *   *

Gniéssin's maternal grandfather was the famous Vilna [1] cantor and wit, Shǎya Fletsinger, nicknamed by the people "Shǎyke Pfaifer" because of his high tenor-ino-altino, suggesting a whistle or a flute.

A charming anecdote exists concerning Shǎyke Pfaifer, of how, in his mature age, he dropped in on a Jewish wedding and asked the guests to collect some money for him; he was being forced into military service, he said. In those cruel days of Nicholas I, it meant twenty-five years of enforced slavery. When the indignant *machatonim,* kinsfolk of the newlywed, refused Pfaifer's plea saying that he was twice a young soldier's age and his story was a lie, he retorted: "Well, this is

[1] Ancient capital of Lithuania.

what has happened. I have a wicked, hateful wife; she has eaten off half of my life (*obgegessen halbe yohren,* in Yiddish), therefore I am to be enlisted again."

This delectable story illumines the knot of paradoxes in which not a single Jewish gift but the very genius of the Jewish people is enmeshed. Pain from the persistent pricks of life—humor and practical joke to neutralize it; bleak travail and affliction, and vitality or self-mesmerism to fight them off.

Ever mangled by the wild leaps of history, by its heinous hammer, the genius of the Jewish people has learned to treat itself to a feast—in the foul dusk of exile. All the sublime concepts and emotions of a genus of spirit *par excellence,* every flame of it, is born in the grey weather of Jewish subsistence, amidst sad and bitter trifles.

Over the murky day of the Amsterdam ghetto, over petty casuistics of old rabbinical ritual, as on a palimsest, are crocheted the great dreams of Spinoza. And the squabbles of Heine with uncle Solomon, and the tragicomical "Commission-house of Harry Heine and Company," a sorry mess, of course, is not this but a stifling corridor leading to the freshness and expanse of the North Sea Cycle?

The thread of spirit looms above the sordid bottom of this life of ours; undulates from Maimonides to Spinoza, from Spinoza to Heine, from Heine to a troubled young musician of our day. *Sursum corda!*—"Our hearts look up!", reads the armorial motto of one of the ancient royal lines of Scandinavia. It is fit to grace the crest of the Hebrew spiritual aristocracy!

I turn the pages of music created by the grandson of a gifted beggar, Shăyke Pfaifer of Vilna, and son of Fabian Gniéssin, a rabbi from Rostov-on-Don.[2] I forget the "wicked wife" or rather the wicked penury of Shăyke Pfaifer and the melancholy druggery of the rabbinical chancery; with a purified joy I breathe the cosmic air of Gniéssin's *Prelude* to Shelley's "Prometheus Unbound":

> There was a change; the impalpable thin air
> And the all-circling sunlight were transformed,
> As if the sense of love, dissolved in them,
> Had folded itself round the sphered world.

In Gniéssin's early songs, Opus 1, published by Biélayev, one finds each ground trait of his mature work: one cannot be mistaken as to their author. The enchanting song *I Ever Dream of the Sea* clasps the best qualities of Gniéssin's gift. Always an original thematic basis; a subtle, and later a more barbed, melodic curve; a bewitching harmony, growing sharp and stringent in his latest work; a delicate polyphony manned through a finely transparent voice-leading. And all this pervaded by a wistfulness, an enigmatic and dolorous drifting.

Gniéssin has travelled far in mastering the technical and artistic means of our time—as they are seen in the remote Russian perspective, of course. His fastidious inflection, harmonic and otherwise, sometimes reach the confines of morbidness, in his *Hymn to the Pest*, for example. His gift has developed, of course, and sharp-

---

[2] One of the principal ports on the Azov Sea.

ened itself, but it clings to the vein already noticeable
in his early work.   About the middle of his creative
route one observes a significant break.   It marks an important change in Gniéssin's artistry, a change caused
by a complete shifting of his creative incentive.

After the loveliest of his early works, the song *Snowflakes,* with its bewitching melodic curve and luminous
harmony, Gniéssin paces swiftly on to a more complex
and radical style.   This leads him through the grey,
sullen shades of his *Sleepless,* admirably in rhythm with
Pushkin's great poem,[3] to the grim *Hymn to the Pest,*
also Pushkin's.   Here happy harmonic *trouvailles* and
an alluring formal shapeliness are sometimes overshadowed by harmonic dreariness, complexity, overdevelopment, also by a neurotic and cerebral preciosity
of diction.   These failings are almost painful in
Gniéssin's incidental music to Alexander Bloch's *Fair-
Show* and in the *Sonata-ballade* for cello and piano.
Gniéssin's peculiar weakness for overdeveloped instrumental interludes between vocal and other soloist
sections, is a relic from this transitional period.

The *Symphonic Introduction* to Shelley's *Prometheus*
marks the first turn of Gniéssin's artistry toward simpler
line; his austere nobility of substance remains intact.
Having gathered, moreover, a religious warmth of tone
and a taste for individualized modal harmony,
Gniéssin's gift has acquired the very means which are
in keeping with the strong personality of the composer,

---

[3] This and other specimens of great Russian poetry can be found in
Poems and Adaptations by Lillian Saminsky.   Oxonian Press, Oxford.
1931.

with his sublimated and sharp individual concept.   His
mature period has given us such luminous music as
Celestial Dew, the song cycle *Consecrations* and the
symphonic dithyramb *Vrubel.*

In Gniéssin's creative self an undercurrent of a racial
mentality is always sensed.   And upon some of his
works, elements of Hebrew melos have been grafted
deliberately.   In these little known pages of enchanting
music, there is a sharp sacramental undertone that
leaves no doubt as to its racial source.   The exquisite
melodic bend fairly burns with an inner exaltation
typical of the Hebraic religious passion.

In Gniéssin's *Celestial Dew* sparkle some traditional
melodic dicta: *Omein* (Amen) in the passage "in the
black ombrage the soul looms illumined and shining";
K'dosh, K'dosh (Holy, holy), after "they glorify the
radiant Creator"; the *duchanen* (ancient motive of the
great benediction of the priests) for the passage "there
is life in death, death fades away and founders".

But the letter of the sacred Hebraic melos matters
little here.

In the very curve and in the swaying of Gniéssin's
melos, in its *duchanen,* in the fanatic flame of *Vrubel,*
we behold the grandson of Shăyke Pfaifer and his canticles, the son of a people who has created the Cabbalah [4]
and the condensed religion of ecstasy, *chassidism.*

And when the artist flees from "the life deceitful and
known into the azure space" (*Vrubel*) and breathes
ecstatically the lofty air of Cosmos, one divines the
shadow of the cabbalist ancestor with his misty thought

[4] Pantheistic dogma of a neo-platonian kind.

of emanation, with his seeking after the Universal Soul that has flung us down to earth as its rays.

* * *

In the creative trend of Alexander Krein, in his tonal self and even in his creative genealogy, there is much in common with Gniéssin.

Krein, too, has passed through a furnace of alien influences—not Wagner's and Rimski-Korsakov's as in Gniéssin's case, but Tschaikovski's and Rachmaninov's, changing later to that of Scriabin and Ravel. Modern musical thought, of which Alexander Krein is surely one of the most gifted messengers, still considers him a progeny of Scriabin.

In the earliest music of Krein, such as the attractive *Arabesque* for piano, as well as in the later fine songs *Autumnal Chant* and *A Seashore Nocturne,* one finds the marks of Gniéssin's work: a peculiar delicacy and expressive elevation, a well-nurtured and telling thematic ground, and notably, an engaging and transparent lyricism that rises to an almost religious pathos.

How significant they seem, these traits, when one recalls the "asemitic" elegies bewailing the sterility and dryness of Jewish musical creation! In these sublime qualities of the two composers one reads again the gentle peculiarities of Hebrew poetic genius, that multichrome and tender soul of a sage gazelle which one discerns lovingly in Heine and Halevi, in Spinoza and Lassalle, in Jesus himself.

And again as in Gniéssin's case, after a certain creative break, the music of Alexander Krein begins to show some new color, a novel and exotic bend, a gravitation toward Hebrew melos, an effort to incept the latter's harmonic aroma and accent.

This new orientation, felt already in some of Krein's earliest pieces, in the captivating *I Shall Weave My Song*, for example, is spurred by his harmonizing of folk-songs. One finds delicate stylization of a Jewish theme in the slow introduction of his *Second Hebrew Suite*, for instance. This new tendency stamps firmly one of the largest of the Krein forms, his orchestral poem *Salomé*. Through the intricate thematic and harmonic tissue of its decidedly modern web, one observes the threads of racial parlance, all thoroughly Hebraic.

The eminent Moscow critic and composer, Léonide Sabanéyev, describes incisively the emotional angles of Krein's Hebraism.

"Krein's emotional plane is characteristic of one of the denominators of the complex Hebraic spirit-uality: it is not its mystic, but its sensual, erotic, earthy facet. Krein loves this passionate, burning earth full of temptation and of fleshly struggle. . . . He is not a religious thinker but an ecstatic; his primeval Hebraic sources are not the grim Prophets but that ancient Hebrew spirit that was ever lured by the bloodstained and sexual cults of the Oriental orgasm." [5]

However, in one of Krein's loveliest creations, in his exquisite song-cycle *Ghazelen* this inflamed sexual thirst undergoes a miraculous transversion. It grows into a melodic pathos almost detached in its sublimity. A

[5] Léonide Sabanéyev: *The Hebrew National School in Music*, Moscow 1924.

bird's singing in the vast azure, a cry lost in a white glow, in distant, untold radiance.

*   *   *

There are several reasons for assigning to Joseph Achron a very special significance.

A Jewish composer who does not wish to pose as a Pole or a Frenchman or a Dane, who insists on representing his own race and blood, such a composer is usually kept in the background. The great Western Forum does not like racial manifestation. Liberalism of the inarticulate kind chooses to silence it; only by clamor can it compel consideration, perhaps. Nor does an artist of a too fastidious sort, with too personal ways and mannerisms, find understanding in this day of vociferous selling of musical wares.

But even the exquisiteness and the aloof peculiarities of Achron's gifts, the uncommon finesse of his tonal perception and his rare technical imagination, retreat before the other merits of the "Achron case".

I do not know of another instance of so complete a change in a composer after striking native subsoil and starting on a second florescence.

One turns the pages of Achron's early violin sonata thick with Russian-German academic paste; one compares it with the aromatic prelude to a later song *Zu dir führt mein Wandern,* or the enchanting, balmy *Canzonetta,* one of the loveliest songs of Israel. One perceives the change in him with joy. It is not even the literal absorption of the lovable Hebrew refrains or the segments of biblical melos that matters. There is a complete transmutation of the composer's æsthetic core.

But in all fairness it must be admitted that in Achron's larger forms, his old academic failings linger on just as do some general drawbacks: overdevelopment; a too sumptuous technical vision which runs away with him; a certain monotonous instrumentalism of thought; something a little facile in his melodic twist.

His *First Violin Concerto* is a very delectable formal conception. Two movements, of which the first pictures a sort of a fantastic cantor reciting and developing some old synagogal or composed patterns; the second deploying an improvisation on two Yemenite folk songs. But this excellent scheme is marred by the usual blunder of the Russian school: to treat episodic and modal material in the stereotyped Western schoolmaster's fashion, overstocking a graceful fluid form with excessive variation, overharmonizing everything, stifling it with enormous technical padding. The second movement of the *Concerto* is more successful; in its grace and neatness of texture and, certainly, in the wonderful expertness of the writing for strings it augurates the adorable *Stempenyou*-suite.

In the *Kinder-Suite,* twenty tonal miniatures for a small instrumental ensemble, the basis of biblical chant (*trop*) does not seem as convincing as one might wish. Some of the miniatures are most alluring in sonority and technical transparency; but as a whole, the piece is over-variated, somewhat obvious and oversweetened. Also it owes somewhat too much and too manifestly to Debussy's and to Moussorgski's children's corners.

In Achron's incidental music to *Golem*, again, all the external paraphernalia of higher Hebraism are found. The biblical chant is utilized, imposing orchestral unisons and open diatonic consecutive fourths are sounded, somewhat ostentatiously, almost to annoyance. These externals ring unreal, mechanical and lifeless. For Achron seeks after the higher Hebraic pathos through technical procedure rather than through spiritual and creative communion.

One feels that the sacramental Hebraic gravity and pathos so native to Gniéssin's æsthetical self, can scarcely be attuned to Achron's nervous tempo, to his rather earthy but alluring vitality. I am not at all convinced that Achron is essentially a *maître* in the Hebraist current of Jewish music. He is infinitely stronger as master of the sublimated and rarified folk-genre, the domestic melos. In the graceful and vibrant and enticingly neat lines of his violin pieces, the *Jewish Dance,* and especially in the *Stempenyou*-suite [6] one joyously perceives the real and best, the supremely inspired Achron.

Even in his fine polyphonic structure, the excellent *Adon Olam,*[7] a fragrant breeze of our sacred song is dampened by his choice of the tonal medium, and by a typically Judaic instrumental and rhythmic lilt.

* * *

[6] Joseph Achron: *Stempenyou* for violin and piano. Universal Edition in Vienna.

[7] Joseph Achron: *Sabbath Evening Service* sponsored by the Choir Committee of the Congregation Emanu-El, New York (Bloch Publishing Company).

In a former book of mine, *Music of Our Day,* I have depicted Milner in the following lines:

> "Milner is a creative force of the first order, very much akin to Moussorgski. He resembles the latter in melodic and dramatic power, but also in technical debilities. He is possessed by the same moving and frenzied humility; he is weakened by the same conceit of an "autodidact", of a self-taught man." [8]

Sharply racial—again like Moussorgski—Milner is naturally less homogeneous, he is less even æsthetically in his larger forms.

In the *Piano Variations* on a folk-theme, both arteries of his creative self show a strange mixture of high spirit and uncouth facility. One finds enticing naturalness of genius, a magical freshness of melodic and harmonic whim—in the lovable fifth variation, for example. And one is dismayed by inspiration of "the least resistance" type, by the facile flow prompted by a pianist's fingers, by the trite chromatic ornament smacking of a schoolmaster's harmony.

Of Milner's larger works, the choral *Unsane Tokef,*[9] especially its first part, is marked by that rarity and sublimity of Hebraic diction which is eminently Milner's own. In his *Psalm XIII* one finds the same spaciousness and dignity, but even more than the

[8] Lazare Saminsky: *Music of Our Day.* Thomas Y. Crowell Company, New York 1932.
[9] Moses Milner: *Unsane Tokef* for cantor and chorus *a capella,* published by the Hebrew Folksong Society in Petrograd and by the "Verlag Juwal" in Berlin and Jerusalem.

Unsane Tokef it is darkened by a tragic ray of desolation.

It is, however, the smaller pieces of Milner that claim, in their emotional loftiness, in their simple grandeur and originality, a place among the greatest songs of humanity. One who has heard *Tanz, Tanz, Meidele Tanz,* (Dance, dance, little girl), a melodic swirl of enchanting agility and delicacy, or *El Hatzipor,* a contour of singular and distant genius, will ever be haunted by these unusual songs, by their termless elevation.

Among the Hebrew composers of today, not even Bloch is capable of reaching this pitch of Hebraic diction or these confines of Hebraic ecstasy.

Part V

AT THE SYNAGOGUE, EAST AND WEST
(Their People and Musicians)

NATIVE SYNAGOGUES OF THE NEAR EAST
AMERICAN SYNAGOGUE MUSIC
A FAMOUS CANTOR

NATIVE SYNAGOGUES OF THE NEAR EAST

AT THE SHRINES OF TIFLIS, CONSTANTINOPLE, SALONICA AND JERUSALEM

Almost all the synagogues of the native communities of Tiflis, a city of great splendor and capital of Georgia and Transcaucasia, are situated in one of its most picturesque quarters. They are built in the ancient trading section, centered about the crossing of the streets of Zion and Jerusalem, near the most sacred Georgian shrine, the ancient Christian orthodox Cathedral of Our Lady of Zion.

The impression of a man chancing here from the West for the first time, is hardly less overwhelming than the sensation of a European traveller who watches the crowd from the Galata bridge, in Constantinople.

Tiny native restaurants, Georgian, Persian, Tartar, Armenian; equally miniature armor shops, money changers' nooks and niches; trading courts with floors covered with precious rugs taken from adjoining shops. Ditch-diggers from Kurdistan with hats shaped like stout reversed jars; Persians from Azerbeidjan—a region on the Caspian Sea—with beards dyed red; magnificent, tall and slender Mingrelians (a tribe from Western Georgia) who drape their bashlyk (cowl) around their heads with a peculiar elegance; old Turkish gentlemen in red fezzes with green foulard gauze wound around their headgear.

But figures of the native Jew, now and then projected on this glamorous screen of an Asiatic capital, often put even these strong silhouettes into shade.

I browsed once near the Georgian Hebrew synagogue, a late afternoon of a Friday, waiting for the *Mincha,* the Sabbath Vespers. Suddenly I stood still in enchantment. I had come upon two splendid, extraordinary figures. They proved to be mountaineer Jews, swordmakers from the wildest corner of Dagestan, a Moslem region on the Caspian Sea.

One of them wore a coat in the form of a woman's *manteau* with large bell-like sleeves, green and trimmed with grey fur; his hat, a green half-globe, also trimmed with grey fur at the base, was similar to the headgear of the Kazan Tartars, from the Volga. The other mountaineer wore something in the nature of a long grey Polish *caftan* with ample, loose hanging sleeves, made of rough canvas; his hat was a sort of a fez, shaped like a round cylinder, also made of pale grey canvas. And, of course,—this is taken for granted in Caucasia—both men wore swords and daggers. These mountaineers were conversing; but this could be guessed only from the slight motions of their heads and their very sparse, almost inaudible words drifting from one to another at long intervals.

Just before the *Mincha,* the evening service, in a small courtyard, formed by the ensemble of synagogue buildings, the *bet-hammedrash* (assembly for biblical study) and various living quarters, several mischievous little girls of Oriental type, dressed in Georgian fashion, began to dance. Others beat the native tambourine for the dancers. I learned from the *shamess* of the synagogue (the beadle) who chased them out, that these were Jewish children. There was nothing in their dress, habits or even type to distinguish them from the Georgian children.

*   *   *

The interior of these native Tiflis synagogues and the prayer-manner is even more stirring than the surroundings.

The synagogue of the Persian Jews is small, dingy, a barn with a tiny courtyard behind it. The women pray either in this court or in its roofed corner, or in the synagogue proper, but in a special enclosure carefully screened. The beards of many of the men are dyed red like those of the Persians from among whom they have recently emigrated. The younger generation, the one born in the Caucasus, drops this Moslem usage. Women, even small girls, dye their hair, fingernails, even their teeth in glowing Titian red.

Some of the women—apparently the most pious ones —approach the *mezuza,* an amulet containing the Holy Name, in the form of a tube nailed up at the entrance, kiss it and weep gently while touching the *mezuza* with their heads.

The service progresses, from the most part, in a majestic stillness very startling to a man who knows the clamorous prayer of the synagogues in Galicia and Southwestern Ukraine. Some prayers, such as *Ata kidashta*

("Thou didst consecrate") recited on Friday evening, are read almost inaudibly, in a sort of ecstatic silence. It is interesting to perceive the similarity of such mode of prayer to the *inner nigun,* the melody sung *within oneself,* of the *chassidim*-sect, the pietists of Austria and Russia. One cannot but consider such a similarity in the prayer-pathos and ritual habits in strikingly dissimilar tribes of the Jewry separated for ages, as another indication of indestructible racial unity.

All prayers at the Persian synagogue are rendered in almost one and the same manner, in the form of a monotonous and melodically vacuous recitative. But now and then, this *melopeïa* branches out into a beautiful pattern. *L'cha, dodi,*[1] the prayer held in special esteem by the Transcaucasian Jews, is sung with such a melodic recitative. And again, it is illuminating to find that this chant resembles our old acquaintance, the traditional *Vaïchulu hashomaim* ("Thus the heavens and the earth were finished", Genesis II, 1) of the European Ashkenasic Jews. The Night-watchman's song from Meyerbeer's *Huguenots* is also an issue of this old synagogal chant. Another illustration of the creative unity of Israel!

When the Friday evening service was brought to a close, the *baal-tefillá,* the "prayer-leader", a volunteer, as they have no regular cantor—a butcher dressed like a well-to-do Persian merchant—approached each one

---

[1] "Come, friend, and meet the bride, Queen Sabbath." This mystical poem written to glorify the union of Israel with our faith, is the creation of the Palestinian poet, Shelomo Al-Kabetz (1505-1572) of Safed. The poem and its chanting has become a favorite sacred song of all Jewish people.

present, and after having kissed the tip of his own fingers, touched the worshippers' fingers. Then he congratulated his fellow-coreligionists upon the advent of the Sabbath.

At the Georgian Hebrew prayer-house one does not find that devout stillness of the Persian synagogue, but again, one is never shocked by anything resembling the nervous noisiness of a Galician congregation. Here, as in the Persian temples, one is captivated by the stern and devout faces of the women, often strikingly beautiful, of an austere and a pure ancient type. On holy days the women drape themselves in their magnificent yellow and black striped shawls. The peaked, conic goat-fur hats of the mountaineers are as striking as their sharply characteristic and heroic faces. The rest of their attire is equally wild. One recalls Cæsar's famous description of the stern and elemental Belgian tribe of the Gauls in *De bello gallico*. He explains that this tribe is so manly and austere because their living in the remote, inaccessible North hinders the merchants from visiting them and selling them wares that tend to effeminate the habits (a naïve anticipation of Rousseau, by the way).

After the last prayer, the cantor, also some Tiflis merchant, approached each old man of the congregation, touched his head with his fingertips and kissed the latter.

* * *

These were the surroundings where I chanced to gather the religious songs of the Georgian Jews.

I began this work in the summer of 1913 as a member

of the Ethnological Expedition of Baron de Guinsbourg. It was not my first journey to the Caucasus, nor my first opportunity to hear the songs of the extraordinary Hebrew tribes of Georgia, Dagestan and Persia. Four years earlier, being enlisted into the military service, I had lived there. But those younger days were completely absorbed in military manœuvers lighted by social amenities and copious festivities, for the people of Georgia, one of the most chivalrous on the face of the earth, treat their foreign guests regally. Also at that period, my interest in Hebrew music had just begun to kindle, and I did not quite gauge the tremendous value of the Oriental-Hebrew music, the æsthetic and scientific vista hidden in its amazing tonal material.

In my work of collecting the Hebrew Georgian chants, I was helped by the *baal krio,* reader of the Scriptures, and the *melamed,* that is, the teacher of the Georgian synagogue's religious school, *haham* David Abramadze; by the son of the chief rabbi of the Georgian Jews, *haham* Malkiel Namtalashvili, and also, by the latter's uncle, *haham* Joseph Namtalashvili. The mountaineer Jews, a tribe of scant culture, bestow the title of *haham,* that is "the wise one", "the learned one", on any man who is somewhat versed in Hebrew learning.

All these men had come from Akhaltzikh, a district, which, as well as the city of Kutaïs and the village Tzhenvǎli—about fifty miles from Tiflis—is the main and the oldest settlement of the Georgian Jews. These assistants of mine assured me that the melodies they imparted to me, had been sung by them since childhood, and that the prayers have been chanted in a similar manner by the Jews of Kutaïs and Tzhenvăli since time immemorial.

* * *

Georgian Hebrew music has three main branches: the purely religious kind including the cantillation of the Bible, semi-religious chants, such as *z'miroth*, festal table songs, and domestic airs, that is, love-songs, wedding tunes, lullabies.

Of all the strictly religious chants I gathered, the two traditional versions of the *Kaddish*, prayer for the dead (the traditional Georgian, *Table I, ex. 7*, and the ancient Akhaltzich versions), together with the chant of the *Shir hashirim, Table I, ex. 2*—the Song of Songs of King Solomon built on a Lydian pentachord,[2] are the most characteristic; they are definitely related to the main type of Jewish religious melody. These three sacred chants are among the most beautiful songs of Israel.

Their *Kol nidre,* based on an Æolian tetrachord, is strange to the Western Jewish ear. Even less typical are the two variants of their *L'cho dodi* built on a hexachord of the harmonic minor; these bear clear marks of Persian influence. One of these variations strongly suggests the enchanting Persian chorus from Glinka's opera *Russlan and Lioudmila*, "Shadows of night cling to the deserted fields"; Glinka did use a genuine Persian folksong. There is nothing surprising in the resem-

[2] This chant is among my *Songs of the Russian Orient.* Universal Edition in Vienna.

blance. Georgia was subjugated by Persia several times, notably during the reign of King Ishmael of Azerbeidjan at the beginning of the sixteenth century and during the domination of the famous warrior, King Nadir-Shah of Persia in the early part of the eighteenth century. Consequently the Georgians have been under strong influences of Persian culture.

To the least characteristic songs manifestly borrowed from the Georgians and very likely also from the Armenians, belong the charming semi-religious air *Deror ikra l'ben imbat* (*Table III, ex. 1*) sung at the Sabbath noon repast; *Yoducha rayonai* (I bless you, my thoughts) traditionally rendered at the *Sudas Abraham*, the Friday evening meal; the Georgian variation of *Zur mishelei ochălnu*, the Sabbath table song, and also a very peculiar domestic air, *Emet ata chatanenu* (You are righteous, O our bridegroom). With the latter melodious address the bridegroom is greeted during the wedding-feast, at the moment of the handing of the wedding-contract, the *Ketuba*.

Turning to the structure and rhythm of this melos one finds the following details.

A number of purely religious, traditional chants, such as the two variants of the *Kaddish* (prayer for the dead) and one of the variations of the *Shir hashirim* (Song of Songs), present a typically Hebrew religious *melopeïa*, a non-measured recitative highly developed and richly ornamented.

The other class of religious chants, manifestly very ancient, being also non-measured recitatives, are marked by a scant melodic development and a short range. They are mostly trichords, built on a three-note scale, and encased in a major third, like the hymn *A solis ortu* of the ninth century sung at the funeral of Charlemagne. Of a similar structure are the Georgian-Persian *Shema Israel*, "Hear, O Israel", (*Table I, ex. 5*) the second variation of the *Shir hashirim* and the cantillation of the book of Esther.

TABLE III.   Songs of the Near East

Caucasian

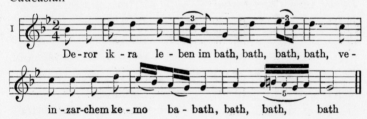

De - ror ik - ra   le - ben im bath, bath, bath, bath, ve-

in - zar-chem ke - mo   ba - bath, bath, bath,   bath

Yemenite

Spanish Hebrew

Ma - ma, si   yo   mi   mo - e - ro,   ma - ma, si

yo - mi   mo - e - ro,   ma - ma, si   yo   mi

mo-e - ro, ha - za - nim no que - ro yo.

Turkish Sephardic

Ya - a - shen al te - ra— deim we - ha - ten

sovit a - le le - - chal ma

le - cha - nir dam - - - mah—

le - cha - nir— dam - mah

Turkish Sephardic

Cantor

A - na be - ko - re - nu— le - ko - ol sha-

The children

ve - nu A - do - nay she - ma— Fine

Cantor   The children

de - va - rim la - kach - ti she - ma, A - do -

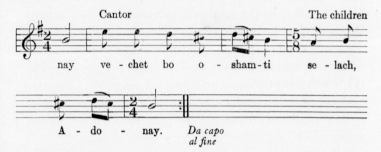

The third structural type includes table-songs, that is "Grace" and other semi-religious chants, and in part, the domestic melodies. They have a clear-cut form-structure dominated by regular, Western rhythmic periodicity.

* * *

This ensemble of observations impels some important conclusions. Of the four modes germane to the Jewish folksong,—the Western European harmonic minor, the Æolian mode, the Myxolydian *Adonoy Moloch* and the common Oriental mode known as *Heijaz*, a slightly modified Phrygian,—only the last is nowhere to be found in the Georgian-Hebrew sacred melos. This means that a typically *Oriental branch* of Israel *knows of no song built on the favorite Oriental scale* seemingly inherent in the domestic song of Jewry-at-large.

Furthermore, the most characteristic and original religious melodies, the very chants used for the traditional prayers and for the cantillating of the Bible, are of Æolian modal structure. Their casting is that of the well known, richly ornamented recitative that is typical of the Hebrew religious song of all lands and all ages. But in the semi-religious and domestic airs of the Georgian Jews, one traces a clear influence of Georgian and Persian music. These airs are dominated by a common harmonic minor mode alien to the Jewish musical mind. It is also significant that wherever this trite scale appears in the Georgian-Hebrew airs, it carries also a rhythmic regularity foreign to Hebrew sacred music.

All these facts bear conclusions on which I have insisted before:

firstly, the Æolian, which is often the mode of the most beautiful domestic tunes of Jewry, is very likely, together with the Myxolydian, the true mode of Hebrew music, of the latter's oldest and purest strata;

secondly, the religious music of Israel, and above everything, the traditional sacred melodies, the chanting of the Scriptures included, should be considered the purest strata of Hebrew music: this sacred melos is the least touched by adoption.

These conclusions are to be read in the typical structure of Hebrew sacred recitative everywhere; in remote Jewish corners, where the tribes have been cut away from the main trunk of the Jewry for untold centuries. In Georgia as well as Yemen.

* * *

The authenticity of the Hebrew Georgian synagogal songs stands also the test of a general historical analysis.

Their link with the general cultural life of ancient Israel is well defined. Historic evidence indicates that the ancestors of the present Georgian and Dagestan Jews appeared in Transcaucasia very early, perhaps even before the destruction of the First Temple. The Georgian and Dagestan Jews consider themselves descendants from the Jewish subjects of King Jehoiakin of Judea and of King Pekah of Samaria, that is, from the Jews carried into captivity after the conquest of Palestine by the Assyrian Kings Shalmaneser (eighth century B.C.E.) and Nebuchadnezzar (eleventh century B.C.E.) .

Archæologists have it that part of the ancient Median kingdom—the present Azerbeidjan region on the Caspian Sea—was thickly populated by Jews, ancestors of the present Transcaucasian Hebrew tribes. The ancient historians also say that this settlement took place before the Christian Era.

It is illuminating to find that the oldest aristocratic Caucasian castes, the princes of Huria, Mingrelia and Cartalinia, bear a striking resemblance to the ancient and proud, purely Hebrew type of Caucasia. In the fifth century C.E., the Georgian sovereigns insisted that their ancestors came from Jerusalem. From then on, the name of David became a favorite with royalty; some of Georgia's great kings have borne the names of "David the Restorer" or "David Bagratide," etc.

Some of the Caucasian tribes, both Christian and Moslem, have preserved old Jewish rites, usages, and even the names of their villages.

The Persian and Arab conquerors were also responsible for the transfer of great masses of Jews to Transcaucasia, between the fourth and eighth centuries C.E. And it is quite likely that the Khazar kings of the Southern Volga *kahanat* (ninth and tenth centuries c.e.) adopted Judaism from the Jewish detachments, ancestors of the Dagestan and Tat Hebrew mountaineers, sent out by the Persian kings of the Achæmenide dynasty to guard the Caucasian-Persian frontier.

Statements in the travel-book of Rabbi Benjamin of Tudela [3] whose journey in the Orient took place between 1160 and 1173, are also significant. He names the Georgian Jews whom he met during his travels, as one of the Jewish tribes who recognize and obey the authority of the Hebrew Prince of Captivity in Bagdad. He points also to the mention in the Scriptures of *Girgasim*, the Georgians.

One aligns these historical data with the pronouncing of Hebrew by the Georgian Jews, and some of their phonetic details, found also in one other tribe of the Hebrew race, the oldest Jewry of upper Galilee. One can then assign to the Hebrew Georgian sacred chant an authenticity and antiquity reliable enough to make it a touchstone for testing any melos that claims to be the old sacred song of Israel.

*　　*　　*

In the enchanting spiritual air of the Georgian-Hebrew synagogue I felt once more the restoring breath of the Jewish religious genius. But I was swayed also by a personal attraction kindled by this noble and vigorous Hebraic atmosphere.

The religious canticle of the Caucasian Jew possesses the same grandeur of substance as does the emotional

[3] *The Contemporaries of Marco Polo.* Boni and Liveright.

air of their prayer. A proud and calm dignity, which a son of the neurotic and tortured Western Israel watches with envy; an exalted stillness; a manly, heroic beauty in the Sephardic dialect of their *loshon kodesh,* of their "sacred language," that is, the biblical Hebrew.

The same tense color, the same force of religious ecstasy one encounters in the poetry and sacred song of the Palestinian Yemenites.

This tribe of Israel was imbedded by Arab conquerors in the Southwestern corner of the Arabian peninsula and has lived there during the last thirteen centuries, lived in a most abject isolation created by bestial hatred of the Bedouin, in an almost complete absence of communication with the rest of Israel. But the poetic and religious Hebrew renaissance, kindled amidst the Palestinian Jewry in the sixteenth century, somehow penetrated to the downtrodden ghetto of Yemen and spurred the creation of the wonderful poems and melodies of the Yemenite Jews.

The British occupation of Arabia during the World War made the Yemenites' life and their migration easier; a steady stream of them is settling in Palestine. In their synagogues and their Jerusalem quarters one admires the ancient burned face which bears an amazing similarity to that of the Byzantine mosaics and ancient Coptic ikons. One drinks in their beautiful, sonorous Hebrew.

Their sacred songs and dances, especially the wedding tunes, are imbued with the same remarkable vitality and expressive might as that of the Hebrew-Georgian song. And curiously enough, among the many traits of resemblance between the Caucasian and the Yemenite Jew, physical and spiritual, is the tendency of their music and poetry to deal with love and wedding themes. On the contrary, the prevalent subject of the Western Hebrew domestic folk-lore is the child; lullabies or children-songs have engaged the tenderest melodic thought of the Polish, Lithuanian and Russian Jewry.

In the chapter "Hebrew Music, Past and Present" of this book, I quote the marvellous religious song *Ani hadal* of the Yemenites. Also, I would like here to point to a magnificent, steel-like melodic line of one of their folk-dances built in a pure Æolian mode (see *Table III, ex. 2*) .

* * *

A sojourn in Constantinople and Salonica afforded me a precious opportunity to meet some of the grand personalities representing the Turkish Sephards of Spanish origin, to listen to their musicians, to record their synagogal chants and their old Castilian and Aragonese ballads.

A reception for foreign guests at the mansions of the two *haham bashi,* the rabbis of Turkey, Mar Haïm Bejarano of Constantinople and Jacob Meïr of Salonica, proved to be the doorway to an acquaintance with the leading men of learning, eminent journalists, diplomats and musicians.

The Chief Rabbi of Turkey, Haïm Bejarano, the more stern of the two divines, was a great leader and savant, an extraordinary linguist, a master of Spanish

But let twelve fair youths surround my death-bed, and leading them—my beloved." [5]

* * *

I secured some other lyric and melodic gems through the gracious courtesy of Isaac ben Elias Navon, son of the rabbi of the Spanish-Hebrew community of Adrianople, the ancient capital of Turkey. This man, of great culture and of a peculiar, dignified gentleness, was an impersonation of that unrivaled old Spanish civility. So may have looked and acted the magnificent Samuel ben Meïr Halevi Abulafia, better known as Samuel Halevi, old Castilian scholar and treasurer to King Pedro the Cruel, friend of the beautiful Maria Padilla and builder of the future El Greco dwelling in Toledo.

In keeping with the poetic and religious emotions of the Oriental Sephardim, the Hebrew Spanish melodic flow has fructified more than anything else, the old synagogal poem of Israel, especially the *piyut* (a derivative from the Greek *poesis,* poetry) and the *selicha,* the supplication.

The synagogal poem, *piyut* whose first blossoming was witnessed in the seventh and eighth centuries C.E., used in its early stages the language and religious symbol of the Bible, but gradually it absorbed the poetic elements of biblical commentators' literature, the Talmudic Mishna. Among the most famous creators of the *piyutim* were Meshullam ben Kalonymos, member of

[5] My arrangement of this song for voice and piano, entitled *Rachelina,* is published by Carl Fischer, New York. It is not a mere harmonization of the folk-air but an art-song freely built over the enchanting pattern.

the noted medieval Roman family; the great Palestinian theologian, Saadia Gaon (tenth century) and the three illustrious Hebrew-Spanish poets and philosophers, Moses ben Ezra, Ibn Gabirol and Jehuda Halevi (eleventh and twelfth centuries). The *selichot* of the Turkish Sephardim are exceptionally beautiful. According to their tradition, the entire month of Ellul preceding the High Holidays, the opening days of the autumn, are given to prayers of repentance—not only the *asseres yemei t'shuvo,* the ten days of repentance that antedate the Day of Atonement. To recite the *selichot* during these ten days only, is a usage among the Jews of the Occident.

One of those traditional *Selichot d'Ellul,* supplications for the month of Ellul, *Yaashen, al teradeim* (*Table III, ex. 4*) is sung at sunrise by the Spanish Sephardim of the oldest synagogues. This melody is greatly loved by the "Spagnols"; at home they play it on a Turkish cither.

An even more uncommon sacred song is *Ana b'korenu,* "Answer our call" (*Table III, ex. 5*), an introduction to the *Selichot de Kippur,* supplications for the Day of Atonement.

*   *   *

This extraordinary melody has archaic traits so strong, that considering the fanatical traditionalism of the Spanish Jews, one is again led to the ancient common root of Jewish music. The ancient features of this song are a purely Gregorian Doric structure and an enchanting antiphony—a responsive singing by the cantor and the children of the congregation who constitute the choir. And just as in the case of the Hebrew-Georgian semi-religious air and table-tune, this melody resembles the latter also in its neat cyclic form of an apparently later origin and in its rhythmic lilt. These traits have surely been assimilated from the dance-song of their former neighbors, the peasantry of Aragon and Castile.

But one discovers even a more direct witness to the close Jewish communion with old Spanish life, of which this picturesque Jewry was part only five hundred years ago.

In a small garden-court of the Salonica Jewish quarter, it was touching to listen to an old *romanza spagnola;* to hear old native Aragon included in the Domain of Israel—*"Aragon i toda la Juderia."* Still, one cannot keep from smiling over these "fields of Israel" when one recalls the vast, hectic camps of Moorish and Jewish traders that were situated outside the huge Spanish city gates, selling every imaginable necessity and luxury imported from Byzance, Arabia, India and even China. Of course, such is a picture of the "fields of Israel" before the expulsion-edict of Fernando the Catholic and Isabella d'Aragon, in 1492.

The ballad is a lament of a Jewish girl carried into captivity by the pirates of Barbary; the text is in the Spanish dialect of the Sephardim of Turkey.

> *"Al rej dellos moror regalo se la jevaria,*
> *Que olvide Aragon i toda la Juderia.*
> *Nia amanessia ni era di dia,*
> *Quando la blanca ninia jorava su manzia.*

O que campos de oliva onde
Mi madre Gracia lavado espandia.
O que pinno ermoso onde mi esposo
Basho su sol ombra azia el su goso."

"To the King of Death she brought herself as an offering so that she might fall oblivious of Aragon and all Israel.   No sooner had dawn begun to glimmer than the white maiden was wailing over her mischance.   O those olive groves where my mother Gracia spread her linen.   And that beautiful pine tree near where my bridegroom sat in his joyousness."

*   *   *

It is instructive to compare the religious chants of the Spanish Sephardim of Turkey with those of Italy.

There one finds the same manly and noble major mode but also the favorite of Jewry-at-large, the *Tefilla* scale, with some minor refractions.   Such, for instance, is the *Shema Israel,* "Hear, O Israel" of the Italian Sephardim recorded in *Libro dei Canti d'Israele,* a book of liturgical chants of the Spanish-Hebrew ritual, by Federico Consolo.[6]   The closing verse of "Who is like unto Thee" is a purely Æolian structure, and the enchanting *Hamavdil*[7] is in a major mode with delightful drifts into sudden and alien inner cadences.

*   *   *

One and the same sound-color, tense and definite, rings in the maze of impressions one gathers from any Jewish conclave in the Near East, be it a synagogal serv-

[6] Published in Florence in 1891.
[7] Number 78 in the Consolo collection.

ice in Tiflis, a young people's dance in the *Mahallé* quarter of Salonica, a *B'nai Brith* musical gathering in Constantinople, a religious feast of the Yemenites in Jerusalem.

Mightily affecting is the resplendent sonority and vigor of the old Sephardic sacred chant; one is absorbed in admiring the proud and beautiful Hebrew tongue, the ancient types, their noble, austere bearing.

Even *a priori,* before settling down to a scientific study of the old Sephardic hymns, one cannot resist the conviction that here, in these dwellings and temples of a remote and a "backward" Jewry, is the repository of the ancient song of Israel.

It is also illuminating to find that it is the great Sephardic Jewry, the Hebrew-Italians, for instance, their past and culture, that forms an extraordinary link between Jewish life and some of the great historical epochs, such as the Renaissance.

One is startled to discover a number of brilliant Jewish musicians of the *seicento* in leading positions at the papal and ducal courts of Italy. Incidentally, two of them, Jacopo Sansecondo and Giovanni Maria employed by Pope Leo X, that magnificent Medici, sat as models for Rafael's Apollo and Sebastiano del Piombo's "violin-player." [8]

One notes with surprise that one of the greatest composers of the Italian Renaissance, Benedetto Marcello, visited the Sephardic synagogue of his native Venice to

[8] The vivacious article by the well-known Prague musicologist, Paul Nettl, *Some Early Jewish Musicians,* published by the "Musical Quarterly" of New York, contains most entertaining material.

look for musical material and a style to which to conform his great choral psalms.

One is even more amazed to follow the career of another brilliant Italian, Salamone Rossi, who styled himself *Shalomo me-haddomim nato a Mantua* (Salomon of the Red Ones, born in Mantua). Between 1587 and 1628 he was the master of music at the court of the Mantua dukes, the favorite musician of Vincenzo II and Vinceno III di Gonzaga, and choirmaster at the Mantua synagogue as well. He is the author of that finely characteristic, famous *Adon Olam*. It is curious to see how Rossi's artistic life was interwoven with that of the grandest composer of Italy and one of the greatest musicians of all time, Claudio Monteverdi, the magnificent and autocratic *maesto di capella* of Saint Marc's in Venice.[9]

Rossi and Monteverdi worked together in Mantua, among other things, on a religious musical drama. Rossi's sister, Madama Europa, a famous singer, participated in the historic première of Monteverdi's *Arianna,* one of the main events in operatic history.

One may rest assured that Monteverdi knew well the great worth of Salamone Rossi and had all possible reverence for him and his Jewish works; he surely listened with admiration to Rossi's performance of his stern and lofty *Adon Olam.*

But the crude ear of the contemporary barbarian and demagogue, corrupted by the new, cheap homophony and the new virtuoso-vocalize of the later Renaissance, was unable to as much as respect those fine old Hebrew

[9] See *Monteverdi* by Henri Prunières.

hymns. Even a musician of finesse, such as Orazio Vecchi, had the vulgar idea of mimicking the Hebrew ritual song in his oratorio-buffa *Amfiparnasso*. This parody may have given Wagner the noble idea to describe the Jewish synagogal music in the neat formula: *"Gegurgel, Gejodel, Geklapper."*

Thus Venice, a narrow stretch of land and water, sheltered Monteverdi, co-worker of a great Jewish musician, full of reverence for the latter's works; Vecchi, detractor of Hebrew musical genius; Marcello, admirer and imitator of Hebrew synagogal music; and Wagner, the dying guest of Palazzo Vendramin, who defiled that noble melos in unspeakable street-jargon.

Even *quot capita tot mentes*—"as many opinions as there are heads" does not explain a mentality wry through racial hatred. Its reasoning has an animal spring; an animal key deciphers it.

AMERICAN SYNAGOGUE MUSIC

In my effort to analyze and to sum up the music sung
in the American synagogue, I do not have in mind those
rare cases when the musical service is directed by men
who know what Jewish religious music is.

There are, indeed, competent and enthusiastic Jewish
musicians who love Jewish music and think it no myth.
I would mention such men as Joseph Yasser, organist
and choirmaster at Temple Rodeph Sholom in New
York, a musician and scholar of outstanding talents and
competence; Reuben R. Rinder, the talented cantor and
music director of the San Francisco Temple Emanu-El;
Emanuel Balaban, a highly gifted conductor and professor of the Eastman Conservatory in Rochester; Jacob
Beimel, the Philadelphian cantor-composer and expert
writer on Jewish musical subjects; the energetic A. W.
Binder of the New York Free Synagogue; Henry Gideon,
director of music at Temple Israel in Boston; Leo Low
and Zavel Zilberts, gifted choir-leaders and composers
of the Brooklyn and Newark communities; Gershon
Ephros, editor of the *Cantorial Anthology,* etc.

That even some of these men should have a mis-
guided or primitive insight into Jewish musical expression is not to be wondered at, for the usual run of
American synagogue music is a rare muddle.

With the exception of some Eastern orthodox religious chants brought into the service without discrimination, American synagogue music is dominated, even partly created, by the non-Jewish organist-choir leader. He is often a mediocre musician and almost always completely ignorant in matters of Jewish music. The average choir leader seldom suspects its existence. Indeed, I do not speak of such excellent and conscientious musicians as the late Frank van der Stucken, Gottfried Federlein, Will MacFarlan or Hugo Grimm, who for many years have been associated with Hebrew musical activities and who have an understanding of Jewish music.

In all fairness one must say that when the organist-choir leader is informed of the existence of Jewish music, he honestly tries to get it for his service. But this very case is the worst. For the variety of sources from which the organist-choir leader of the American synagogue draws his material, makes of the synagogue musical service of this country an extraordinary concoction, deprived of root, of style and of unity.

*　*　*

Three elements can be discerned in American synagogal music.

One is borrowed from the European and Eastern Jewish tradition, more often from the pseudo-tradition. The second element is the formidable volume of second-rate church music, artificially accommodated to the synagogue service. It is totally foreign to the spirit of the Hebrew prayer, to the pathos and color of the *loshon kodesh*—the "sacred tongue." And then, there is a thin and pale layer of so-called American Hebrew religious music.

Let us scrutinize closely all the three elements.

The ignorance of the choirmaster or cantor has sanctified as traditional many hymns created or adapted by Jewish "classics of the synagogue," such as Sulzer or Levandowski. Thus Sulzer's *Mi chomocho* in d major composed for his *Yomim neroim* service (part of the *Shire Zion,* High Festival's service) , is now considered traditional. Nobody would dare to replace it by another *Mi chomocho,* a more vigorous and characteristic one. The curious thing about it is that Sulzer adapted the old synagogal melody of *Bor'chu* and made it, with an utter neglect of sacred tradition, into a *Mi chomocho.* And it is quite probable that this chant derives from the church canticle *Iste Confessor* of Paul the Deacon, of the ninth century.

To realize how perfectly absurd is the halo of tradition crowning some of the sacrosanct American synagogal hymns, it is enough to know that the "traditional" *En kelohenu* (None is like our God) , is an old German song, *Grosser Gott, wir loben Dich;* and the "traditional" *Rock of Ages* (the *Mooz tzur,* old Hanukkah tune) ,[1] is simply Martin Luther's own *Nun freut Euch, Ihr liebe Christen.*

There are even more comical claimants upon the sanctity of tradition. Sulzer's *Hayom t'hamtzenu,* the hymn closing the Yom Kippur afternoon service, is the German ditty:

---

[1] Hanukkah is the Feast of the Maccabees.

"Auf der grüenen Wiese
Hat er mich gefragt;
Liebst Du mich, Louise?
Hat er mir gesagt!

Really, if according to Wagner and Chamberlain, the Jews have contaminated Aryan music with their accent and wailing, it is "tit for tat," for the Aryans have contaminated our synagogue with some most shallow airs.

The American synagogue service is full of such nonsense, tradition created by ignorance. As a matter of fact, excepting the oldest Hebrew melodies like the ancient *Yisgadal, Shema, Geshem* (or *Thal*) , and the cantillation of the Bible, no Hebrew song can be considered traditional in the true sense of the word. Only the last named chants of our synagogue have a fixed place in the service; they are traditional in the same sense as are the ancient hymns of St. Ambrose of Milan or of Pope Gregory. Still, the worst thing in the *would-be* traditional Jewish music or traditional style, is an adaptation of the cheap and maudlin type of the Eastern religious music, with its Oriental platitudes and banal minor.

One of the greatest absurdities of American synagogal music is, for instance, the stylizing of our most vigorous prayers, like the *Kedusha* or *Toras Adonay,* in that unbearable, tearful minor mode.

The really traditional Jewish music, the cantillation of the Bible—such fragments of it as the wonderful *coda jubilans* of the Book of Genesis, *V'Noah motzo chen b'ene Adonay*—are built in a major mode. They are heroic and jubilant of nature, of the same character as the traditional conclusion of the Scriptural texts, *Hazak, hazak, v'nischazak* (*Table I, ex. 8 and 8a*).

This element and its style should prevail in the Sabbath service. If no more suitable music can be found, it would beseem the Sabbath infinitely better to have the joyous and powerful *Hallelujah* of Purcell or *O Judah, rejoice,* from Handel's *Maccabeans,* or other vigorous work of a great European classic, rather than to sing absurdly effeminate and orientalized tearful *Kedushas* of modern make. They are an offence to the spirit of the Sabbath.

Here again, both forces, the Jewish "modern" synagogal composer and the organist of sundry denominations, have managed to pile up mountains of their own plaintive *Kedushas* and other hymns; they fairly flood the American synagogue service.

Another element which has nothing to do with the spirit of the Hebrew prayer and is a disgrace æsthetically, is the third rate church song adapted by our service as a closing hymn and anthem.

Why should not the Friday night service follow the indication of the Prayer Book? Why should we not always sing then the *Adon Olam* or for that matter, the *Yigdal?*

One finds fine settings for these great hymns of our faith among the works of Salamone Rossi, Sulzer, Gerovitch and Spicker. But here again, the habitual choirmaster conducting the music of the synagogue has too little feeling for and understanding of the Hebrew prayer; and eager to please the congregation rather than to lead them, he gradually transforms the closing hymns into a form of entertainment.

Our Hebrew creed has not yet found a leader authoritative enough and conscious enough of the great place music has or should have in the religious ceremony, to interfere strongly and efficiently as did Pope Pius X with the musical ritual of the Roman Church. This enlightened Pontiff rendered a great service to his church, and a no lesser one to musical culture in general.

A quarter of a century ago he issued the famous encyclical *Motu Proprio* ordering that Catholic church music be purged of all the trash that was clogging its pure flow, and that the ancient Gregorian chant be given again a dominant part in the service.

In this country Cardinal O'Connell, the Archbishop of Boston, has drastically forbidden the use of trashy and sentimental church hymns of "modern" make, so well liked by congregations. The valiant Cardinal dubs this literature "sob-stuff." Also, President Wilson, when Governor of New Jersey, asked the Protestant church to condemn this kind of ecclesiastical song.

In his *Protestant Church Music in America,* Dr. Archibald I. Davison of Harvard University remarks with telling precision the domain of true religious music: "I firmly believe that the validity of church music depends upon the completeness with which it abjures all the personal and the secular elements of concert performance."

Dr. Davison would not permit solo singing, even that accidental to an anthem, would not tolerate a quartet.

The Hebrew American communities should follow leaders of such rigid taste and judgment.

I wish to say, however, that my objections pertain only to the cheap kind of the so-called "modern" church songs which have slipped into the synagogue and are an insult to both the synagogue and the church. Great religious songs set by masters of the past, should assuredly be sung in the synagogue, in proper place. This classical music interprets the spirit of our psalm and prayer with much more fidelity and enthusiasm than mediocre or cheap "modern" Jewish synagogal composition. I would rather see an entire Sabbath service sung to the music of Bach, Handel and Mozart than to listen to that abomination, patronized by the American Synagogue, the Schlesinger service, or that extraordinary symposium of musical mediocrity exhibited in our Union Hymnal.

At the Temple Emanu-El of New York, whose music I have the honor to direct, we use for the hymn placed by the Union Prayer Book before the *Olenu l'shabeach* (the Adoration) the fine chorals of Bach, Handel, Arcadelt, Purcell, Palestrina together with Jewish religious songs, traditional with the various branches of the Jewry.

That hymn before the Adoration is the natural and the best place for singing appropriate choral works by great classical masters, including, of course, the great Jewish composers, Meyerbeer, Mendelssohn, Halevi, Rubinstein.

That very strange musical mixture, and one of recent make, the American synagogal music, is often but a habit

grown from using certain hymns for two or three generations. Thus, for instance, a banal *I Lift Mine Eyes* of
Alois Kaiser, has for years opened the New Year's service
in many synagogues. The Vesper Service of *Yom Kippur*
is opened in many temples not by the glorious *En
komocho* by Sulzer, but by Spicker's *None is like unto
Thee,* an adaptation from *Freischütz,*—an odd idea,
indeed.

Still, this is not nearly as grotesque as the feat told of
by Dr. Davison: "In one Episcopal church it is the in-
variable Easter custom to replace the *Gloria in Excelsis*
by "The Lost Chord" played on the trumpet." [2]

I am sorry to criticize the late Max Spicker, my prede-
cessor at Temple Emanu-El of New York, who was an
earnest and noble human being, devoted to his duty and
an excellent musician; but he had no knowledge of Jewish music, nor any flair for it. The man whose *Synagogal Service* constitutes the staple food of the American
synagogue, whose music is becoming *the* American
Hebrew musical tradition, had very strange ideas. His
Kedusha is built on a motive taken from Wagner's
Rienzi, and he himself naïvely makes a proud note
about it in his service.

Roots, unity and style are sorely needed by American
synagogue music; and above all a communion with true
synagogal melody. I must say, however, that on the
whole, the leading Reform Congregations of the United
States do their best to bring back the old Hebrew musical tradition and to cultivate it anew. These Congrega-

[2] Archibald T. Davison: *Protestant Church Music in America.*   E. C.
Schirmer, Boston 1933.

tions show a true respect for our old synagogal song; their leaders thus reveal themselves as men of taste and culture.

* * *

The synagogal music of this country, a veritable asylum of mediocrity for generations, a machine-made everyday utility, has begun to show of late quite remarkable symptoms of florescence. And the *Sacred Service,* music for the Sabbath morning ritual, by Ernest Bloch, a mighty utterance of Israel's tonal genius, newly awakened, is far beyond anything yet conceived within the shrines of American Israel.[3]

What strikes one in Bloch's liturgy at the outset is a cleansing of his musical speech from much of that well known plaintive and insipid Oriental *melopoeïa* which passes for Jewish music, and which marred Bloch's former Hebraic style.

The very opening of the service, a crystalline, gently lit prelude to "How lovely are thy tents, O Jacob" presents a novel Bloch. Here is music of a sunny evenness, reflecting an unruffled old creed and a sturdy racial allegiance.

In this opening hymn as well as in the text of his *Sacred Service,* Bloch uses the famous Gregorian pattern worked so wonderfully by Mozart in his finale of the *Jupiter* symphony. Of course, Bloch has a dual idea: first, to infuse into his new building material the primeval vigor and serenity stamped on the Gregorian

[3] Ernest Bloch: *Avodath Hakodesh* (Sacred Service). C. C. Birchard and Company, Boston 1934. The Bloch service is sponsored by and dedicated to Gerald F. Warburg, the well-known American musician.

chant; secondly, to point once more to the latter's well-known source, the ancient Temple chant of the people of Israel.

The following two antiphonal chants where the choir —and presumably the congregation—responds to the profession of creed uttered by the cantor, are set in bold contrast as to their religious expression and the tonal-declamatory form.

"Praise Ye the Lord", in the powerful biblical Hebrew *Borechu et Adonaï hammevorah,* is tonally translated by Bloch into a formal act of ritual, an invocation; whereas *Shema Israel* (Hear, O Israel, the Lord Our God is One) , progenitor of *Credo in unum Deum,* has an awed gleam of cognizance of the Supreme Force that clasps the Universe into oneness.

It is curious that Bloch's musical counterpart of these two "laudations" are conceived in an order that reverses the traditional musical expression given by the synagogue to these texts. It is Bloch's *"Praise the Lord"* that bears the mighty tribal countenance. His "Hear, O Israel", with its predominant mystical piano, rings like an annunciation of the mystical wedding of the Creed and Israel—a favorite Hebrew vision—rather than like an impetuous, race-urged profession of faith, *urbi et orbi.* Such intensified stress marks the traditional musical run of "Hear, O Israel", as conceived by the so-called classics of synagogal music.

The next laudation, "Who is like unto Thee amidst the mighty, O Lord, extolled in praises, Master of wonders," is ecstatic to the extent of roughness; neither is it free from shrill, neurotic orientalism. But its best, the closing section *Adonaï yimloch* (The Lord will reign forever and ever), reaches a more elevated pitch of religious and tonal radiance while remaining just as charged with ecstatic might as is the opening.

I remember a Vesper service sung by a chorus of pilgrims supported by that unforgettable, almost human voice of the famous organ at the Cathedral of Seville. And I recall the extraordinary fervor of the praying multitude at a pontifical mass at the Cologne Cathedral, on a divine Sunday morning in May. This *Adonaï Yimloch* of Ernest Bloch approaches such a condensed, volcanic ecstasy of the faithful, as the intoxication experienced in the shrines of Cologne and Seville.

*   *   *

After the quiet and mournful soliloquy "O Rock of Israel," where the temporal, the human, the narrowly Jewish again filters through the sturdy frame, comes, perhaps, the most beautiful portion of this *magnum opus* of Ernest Bloch, the *Kedusha,* Sanctification.

Here the cantor solo "We hallow Thy Name in eternity" is of unearthly enchantment. Its music has the stillness, the delicate glow of pathos that reminds one of the hymn of the early Christian hermits.

"Blessed are the silent ones. Blessed are those who build walls of stillness around themselves. They do not argue, nor do they probe Thy holy mysteries. Blessed are those who sing before Thy face, O Lord, like a lyre."

And to this seraphic song of Israel answers again a savagely ardent, tribal outburst, *Yimloch Adomaï le'olam*

(May the Lord reign forever). Its barbaric dance-like commotion brings to my memory the dervish-like rites and furor of a chassidic sect from Karlina, in Galicia, who at the Feast of Tabernacles nearly wrecked their synagogue with their ecstatic religious dancing.

Bloch's response to Silent Devotion, "May the words of my mouth be acceptable to Thee, O Lord, my Rock and my Redeemer" is an infinitely gentle interlude. It is an intimate tonal confession, like one of those "inner songs" (*ein inner Nigun*) of the Hebrew chassidic sectarian, intoned in utter stillness, almost within themselves. Man dwells in his dark corner with only a glimmer of faith to trace the Door of Redemption.

And again, with a savage, tensely pitched force, storm in the two great hymns, "Lift Up Your Head, O Ye Gates" and "Thy Glory Is in Heaven and in the Earth." Two mighty waterfalls that flank a peaceful mountain slope, they supply the introduction and closing cadence for the reciting of the Bible.

The *Olenu* (Let us adore the ever-living God) returns to us that adorable, serene golden light of a Sabbath morning which stilled our heart in the initial "How lovely are thy tents, O Jacob." And then comes the closing segment of the service, the prayer for the dead (Kaddish) and the *Adon Olam* (Master of the Universe), an integral part of the Hebrew ritual, a poem written by an unknown Hebrew-Spanish poet in the twelfth century.

Here emphatically we find the former Bloch, the one so well described in Leigh Henry's admirable words, "Bloch is the voice of Israel's awe and tribulation. . . .

For him existence seems a time of probation. The austere spirit of Bloch awaits the Jewish millennium, and therein the Day of Judgment." [4]

This vigorous work by one of the foremost masters of our time is in every respect destined for and will fare best in the synagogue.

The Sacred Service has also a concert version, for solo, chorus and orchestra. It is my impression that the orchestra helps to overstress the super-emotional parts of the service and to sharpen that climactic tempestuousness which smacks of the ordinary.

The synagogue will subdue the over-exuberant and the superficial quasi-tribal climaxes, will lend dignity and pathos of quality to the rendition.

The orchestral accompaniment, whose outbursts only accentuate the high theatrical hue of some of the over-stressed passages, will be felicitously eliminated in the synagogal presentation of the Service. This in turn will tend to give the rendition its proper line and proportion.

Then the full value of this important work will benefit Judaism, the synagogue and our every-day cultural life.

[4] Leigh Henry: *Two Hebrew Composers*, Musical Standard, London, 1925.

A FAMOUS CANTOR

Eliezer Gerovitch of Rostov

One Jewish profession exists, whose traits and even welfare history seems to have been unable to improve. The position and the spiritual air of the *chazzanuth* (the cantorate) seem to have remained unchanged during the thirteenth, the fifteenth and the nineteenth centuries, during the age of Emanuel of Rome, of Hertz Treves and of Nissan Beldzer or Gerovitch.

The famous Emanuel, Jewish poet and a citizen of Rome, has portrayed his contemporary, the thirteenth century *chazzan*, i.e., cantor, very vividly. As a poor devil and *shlim-mazel*, a luckless and ignorant creature, humiliated by and given crumbs from the opulent table of his congregation; yet capable of lifting the latter and himself to high ecstasy when possessed by inspired song.

Now and then, through all ages, one finds, of course, cantors who were men of learning and high culture. The renowned Maharil, Rabbi Jacob Levi Mölin of Worms (1356-1427), was equally great as a rabbi and cantor, and he left important traces in both rabbinical learning and synagogal music.

In our own time men like Pinchas Minkovski of Odessa, A. Z. Idelsohn of Cincinnati, Jacob Beimel of Philadelphia, Moshe Rudinov of the New York Temple Emanu-El, and several other cantors, command respect by their reverent musicianship and knowledge. But as a rule, the *chazzanuth* of our day presents the same picture of distress, ignorance and bad taste as it did in the Middle Ages.

Rabbi Hertz Treves, rabbi and cantor in Frankfurt am Main (1470-1550) has this to say concerning the *chazzanim:*

> "They have ceased to be writers of the Torah (Bible), *Tefillin* (phylacteries containing the Holy Name, attached to the forehead and right arm for morning prayers) and *Megilloth* (script of the book of Esther). Nor do they care for the correct grammatical reading, or for the meaning of the prayers. They are concerned only with their songs, and have no regard for the real sense of the words. They neglect the traditional chants of their ancestors." [1]

Our own time represented by a highly gifted and learned musician, Cantor Eliezer Gerovitch, does not alter the tenor of complaints uttered by the medieval Hebrew divines.

There is, indeed, an extraordinary kinship between Rabbi Hertz Treves' admonition and the moving petitions of a remarkable human being and a master of synagogal music, Eliezer Gerovitch. Gerovitch's words were few, and they were uttered long ago. But their import is as alive and as impelling today as when they were spoken—half a century earlier. And their stern message has the same meaning for any of the great Jewish congregations—whether in Paris, New York, or

---

[1] A. Z. Idelsohn: *Jewish Music,* Chapter XI.

Berlin—as it had then for the obscure *kehilah* of Rostov-on-Don in southern Russia.

* * *

Eliezer Gerovitch was born in 1844 in a Ukrainian townlet. His father, a *maskil,* adherent of the then new striving to taste of the European culture of their Christian neighbors, himself taught little Eliezer Russian and German. He studied the Scriptures and Talmud with the rabbi—also cantor—of the village, Reb Nuchim Osher, a man of rare spiritual purity and an inspired singer, who was adored by his pupil. Gerovitch's synagogal collections, *Shirei Zimro* and *Shirei Tefilos,* contain several synagogal songs of Rabbi Nuchim, harmonized by Gerovitch.

Against his father's wishes, Gerovitch emigrated to Odessa to cultivate his beautiful voice, to study *chazzanuth* under the famous cantors Blumenthal and Spitzberg, the latter a pupil and propagandist of Sulzer. Gerovitch entered also a musical theory class at the Odessa School of Fine Arts. He joined later the Petrograd Conservatory and worked under such great singers as Cotogni and Masini, but resisted all offers from the operatic stage.

He decided to devote his life to *chazzanuth* and synagogual composition; it was at the synagogue of Rostov-on-Don that he achieved distinction as a master of synagogal music.

Already during his student-life, in Odessa, there was a growing tendency to fight the "popular," the cheap and pleasing musical elements of the services; also to resist the influence of Sulzer whose style amounted to a mediocre imitation of Catholic and Protestant music.

Gerovitch turned resolutely to the old traditional Hebrew melody. His harmonization he kept transparent and close to the spirit of the old Jewish song.

However, in spite of his prominent position in the Jewish and Christian musical world, all his life he had to fight the peculiar taste and demands of his congregation. Only during his later years did he see his authority become impregnable.

* * *

A touching document is left us, a fragment of Gerovitch's letter to his congregation which reflects his struggles and grief. The simplicity and majesty of this remarkable address strikes one as well as the aloofness and firmness of the æsthetic position of this admirable musician who had divined the true way of our sacred music. One is moved deeply by the hidden suffering of an artist whose pure and inspired work was daily upset by ignorant, or worse, indifferent hands.

"I see lately," wrote Gerovitch, "that you demand a new kind of singing in our synagogue. Evidently, my strict, truly sacred style, the stately and noble order established by me in our musical service, does not seem to you entertaining enough. You think that my style is old, and the style of the new cantors and composers is more becoming to our elegant new *Schul*.

"But this is a bitter mistake. The cheap tunes of our younger cantors I have heard as long as sixty years ago in Eishishki.[2] The only difference in our modern cantor is that he uses the cammerton, wears a pastor's vestment and a biretta, whereas the *chazzanim* from Eishishki wore, during the service, a simple *caftan* and a skull-cap and wrapped themselves in a *talis*.

"My noble recitatives are the true synagogal singing. Of course, the Western European cantors also cultivate this style, but they have edited these old traditional songs so drastically that almost nothing Hebrew is left of them.

"Many times I spoke to the young cantors who came to acquaint themselves with my work, and I pleaded with them to leave their rubbish and to sing our stately old sacred songs. These cantors always answered in the same way. They detest their own rubbish and recognize my singing as the very thing to be introduced at every decent synagogue; but *what is one to do with the Jews who like that agreeable rubbish?*

"Please, honorable gentlemen," says Gerovitch to his congregation, "do not give my colleagues, the cantors, a reason for saying the same thing of our own congregation. For twenty-seven years I have endeavored to refine the taste of our worshipers, and I have succeeded. For God's sake, do not destroy my creation on which I have labored so long."

It is interesting to note that at the time when this noble epistle was written, Gerovitch had already enjoyed an extraordinary prestige in the world at large. Luminaries of the Orthodox Greek-Catholic church such as the great Russian church composer, Archangelski, the Armenian Archbishop Kevork, the Deacon Sytchov, music director of the Russian orthodox archbishopric,

2 A small Ukrainian town.

already held Gerovitch in great esteem and sought his musical advice.

At the celebration of the 70th birthday of Cantor Gerovitch, Deacon Sytchov formed a special choir, composed of choristers from the synagogue and the orthodox Russian Cathedral and performed ten synagogal works of Gerovitch.   He died in 1913.

On reading Gerovitch's pathetic lines, one is irresistibly tempted to recall a quite different and remote historic figure, that of the greatest musical genius of the Italian Renaissance, the all powerful Cantor,—cantor meant then music director—of the great Cathedral of St. Mark in Venice.   I speak of Claudio Monteverdi (1567-1643).

On following the pulsating and multicolored career of Monteverdi, described so admirably in the book of Henri Prunières, eminent Parisian writer and editor of the *Revue Musicale*,[3] one marvels at the amazing power bestowed on Monteverdi by the grandees of Venice who managed the administration at St. Mark's Cathedral.   These mighty and dreaded *procuratori* had grasped the full extent of Monteverdi's genius and lent him every possible aid in following his lofty ideals.

How fortunate would it have been if Eliezer Gerovitch's congregation had had even a shade of such reverence for *their* master of music!

* * *

The distinguished Russian Hebrew composer, Michael Gniéssin, has brought forward some interesting points

[3] Henri Prunières: *Monteverdi*, English edition by E. P. Dutton, New York 1926.

in regard to that extraordinary spirit and grandeur that permeated Gerovitch's idea of a task, at once priestly, interpretive and creative. Both the personality of Gerovitch and Gniéssin's comment seem to us of another world.

There is among some Jewish intellectuals an erroneous idea that the Jewish worshiper has not enough reverence for the synagogue. The Eastern synagogue, Polish, Russian, Galician, is found to be quite noisy and somewhat disorderly, shocking to compare with the temples of other creeds. As to the Western Reform temple, its fault is—too little appreciation of the synagogue as the source and carrier of our musical art. Let us say, however, in passing, that while we condemn the synagogue for the assimilation of alien sacred art, we should not close our eyes to our temples' fostering of the old Hebrew chant.

But to overstress the sacredness of the synagogue is wrong, continues Gniéssin. As a matter of fact, the synagogue is not really a temple; it is only a temporary shelter of the cult, a temporary house of Hebrew sacred learning.[4] Once our people possessed but *one* Temple. But the synagogue was not successful in trying to play the rôle of *the* Temple. This is how the synagogue has come to be criticized.

When our future and true temple will spring up, it

[4] The latest discoveries of Hebrew archæology seem to support this view. In his *Ancient Synagogues in Palestine and Greece* (Oxford Press) Dr. E. L. Sukenik of the Hebrew University in Jerusalem points to the "scholars who claim a pre-Exilic origin for the synagogue and who believe that houses of prayer and study existed in Palestine side by side with the First Temple and its sacrificial ritual,"

will be also a seat of our renascent and true Hebrew musical art. This temple, the future synagogue, will be the carrier of the highest art, a shrine where the supreme achievements of our creed will cross with the pure stream of our reborn sacred melos.

In a way, these colorful opinions of Michael Gniéssin conform with the historic development so forcefully traced by Dr. Kaufmann Kohler in his *Origins of the Synagogue and the Church.*

The very origin of the synagogue as an institution where the worship and the creative forces of the laity were to mitigate and to supplement the aloof, self-contained priesthood,—this historic picture is in full accord with the idea of a new consecration springing from the religious folk-melos and its servitor, the cantor.

Gerovitch, a cantor of the most elevated type, a priestly and exalted voice of prayer, he it is, who was really slated to be the cantor for the temple of our religious art, the champion of the purification of the synagogal melos.

*   *   *

As a composer and builder of a Hebrew art, Gerovitch, as I have said before, was also particularly fit for the sheer musical work of extracting, bringing to light and fostering the pure, ancient elements of Jewish religious music. His correct racial-artistic instinct drew him past everything alien, in his own composition, and during his later life Gerovitch shared in the stand taken by the young composers of the Petrograd Hebrew Folk-song Society.

He was actively aware of the significance of the old synagogal recitative and the traditional chant as the sole true basis for the renascence of Hebrew sacred music. His later works are often built on the old Hebrew modes, in his *Vayi binsoa,* for example, of *Yisgadal v'yiskadash* from the fourth volume of his synagogal collection *Shire Zimroh.* He reintroduced the use of the archaic *Adonoy moloch*-mode clearly understanding its stylistic value for the reborn synagogue music. True, he also shows a weakness for the *Aavo rabo* mode, in his arrangement of the old *Yigdal,* for instance.[5]

He inaugurated the modal harmonization of the traditional chant knowing that this is the only correct treatment of old melodic material which shuns the Western major and minor. In his compositions Gerovitch used also fragments of the ancient biblical cantillation; his original *L'cho Adonoy* (Thine is the glory) from the *Shire Zimroh* is entirely built on the *taamei neginoth.*

Why, then, was not this man definitely cast for important action in Hebrew religious art? Why was he not given the power to effect the complete turn of tendency in synagogal music, the upturn so eagerly expected?

In his papers on Gerovitch, Michael Gniéssin indicates only one cause of this failure. The creative activity of Eliezer Gerovitch coincides with a turning moment in the history of synagogal music. His creation could not possibly have reached the oneness which

---

[5] I have re-edited and rearranged Gerovitch's version of the *Yigdal,* which is lacking in contrast, in my *Holiday Services* (Bloch).

marks work born in organic epochs when each composer is thoroughly strengthened by generations of predecessors.

Indeed, one must grant that the latest organic epoch called upon to renovate synagogal music began to pulsate only in recent years, with the birth of the neo-Hebraic musical current. Gerovitch was too old to become a leading champion, the mouth-piece and warrior of this movement.

But there was an even greater obstacle to Gerovitch's leadership. He did not wholly grasp the importance of the theoretical side in the coming reform of synagogal music; he did not realize the necessity of a discriminative analysis of the new technique.

Gerovitch's cantorial recitatives and many of his fine, stately chorales are invariably individual and rich melodically, full of refreshing modal turns and of harmonic *appperçus*. But while he clearly visions the new art—heaven opened up by the new cultivation of the old sacred recitative—he does not seem to be able to appraise and to regulate the use of its various elements, very uneven as to their artistic and racial value. The harmonic and melodic potentialities of the Hebrew ancient chant he employs casually, in a sort of groping in the dark.

His conscious taste for modal harmonization was not strengthened by a sure, theoretically justified choice of the modes and the harmonic style related to the renascent idiom of the pure and elevated, true type of Hebrew sacred music.

However, even though the musical art of the synagogue still waits for its great reformer, for the man who will mold into oneness all the achievements of the new era of Hebrew tonal art, the name of Gerovitch must still be retained by history as that of a highly gifted cantor-composer, as that of a standard-bearer of a movement that has led to a renaissance in Jewish music.

BIBLICAL MELODY

Cantillation of the Scriptures, the *taamim* or *neginoth*, is one of the oldest monuments of Israel; it is closely interrelated with both Jewish and Christian music. A study of the biblical chant is, therefore, of the highest importance from each of these three angles:

  a) the facts relating to this biblical melody, to its age and structure;
  b) the link with early Christian church music;
  c) the historic and æsthetic fate of the biblical chant.

————————

Exact notation of melodic steps and intervals did not appear before the eleventh century when Guido d'Arezzo originated his method of writing down music.

However, even in earlier times indirect and loose methods of musical notation existed: letters corresponding to definite notes in ancient Greece, and *neumes* or signs in ancient India, Judea and Armenia. The neumes signified the rise and fall of the voice, the melodic curves and other details of the chanting. They helped the singer to recall the vocal turn. The neumes originated in and later totally replaced *cheironomy*, the ancient system of finger-motion and gesture used by the presbyter or the levite to indicate the melodic rise and fall of the chant. Analysis of the basic and the oldest neumes of India, Judea, Byzantium and Armenia re-

veal a remarkable similarily in their hieroglyphic por-
traiture of vocal turns.

Cheironomy (Greek *cheironomia,* hand-signs) can be
traced to ancient Egypt; it is found on the frescoes
within the pyramids. Cheironomy was in use in Palestine during the first centuries c.e. The great Talmudist Rashi[1] saw in France and Germany, as late as the

TABLE IV.   Biblical Cantillation.

An Ashkenasic silluk.   A variation

Some phonemas, from the Pentateuch cantillation.

Mer - ho tip - ho mu nah es - nah - to, mer - ho tip-

ho mer - ho sof po - suk.   kad - mo ma - pakh   pash - to

mu - nah   ko - ton mer - ho tip - ho   es - nah - to

---

[1] Talmud is a compilation of commentaries on the Bible made
through the ages by great Hebrew theologians. One of the greatest
among them, Solomon ben Isaac or *Rashi,* who was born in 1040 and

Old French cantillation

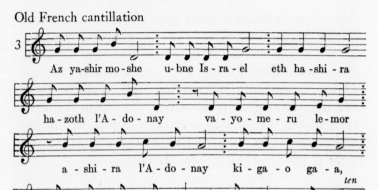

Az ya-shir mo-she   u-bne Is-ra-el   eth ha-shi-ra

ha-zoth l'A-do-nay   va-yo-me-ru   le-mor

a-shi-ra   l'A-do-nay   ki-ga-o   ga-a,

sus ve-ro-che-vo   ra-ma   ba-yam

eleventh century, some visiting Palestinian precentors who used hand-signs while chanting the Bible. Sources even older than Rashi contain the description of Hebrew cheironomic gestures, such as the fast trembling movement of the hand interpreting the neume known as *shalsheleth,* that is "chain" or "zigzag." Such signs are still employed by the Jews of Yemen in Arabia.

In his admirable treatise on scriptural cantillation [2] Dr. Oscar Fleischer tells very colorful stories concerning the famous St. Gall school of plain-chant singing, where, also, as late as in the eleventh century, cheironomy was still in use. Some of these tales point to the great reverence in which the traditional cantillation was held. Of course, the situation was not different in the Jewish world.

died in 1105 c.e. in Troyes, France, was the head of the great rabbinical schools in Champagne.

[2] Oscar Fleischer: *Neumen Studien,* Breitkopf and Hartel, Leipzig 1895.

In 1030 Emperor Conrad Hohenstaufen, surrounded by his barons and princes of the church, celebrated Easter in Ingelheim. The service was conducted and sung by the famous Ekkehard of St. Gall, cantor of the Mainz Cathedral. When after the *Alleluia Pasca nostrum* the cantor lifted his hand "to design the musical sequence to be sung," three bishops rose humbly amidst the choir, to take part in the singing. They were pupils of Ekkehard at St. Gall.[3]

Hebrew written literature began to employ the sign-system, roughly speaking, after the Babylonian Captivity. Some historians think that this system was established by the Great Assembly, *K'nesses haggedolo,* the same rabbinical convention that formulated the liturgical text of the *Sh'ma Israel* (Hear, O Israel), *Kedusha* (Sanctification) and *Shemone Esre,* the Eighteen Benedictions. (All of these are important parts of the Hebrew ritual.)

This famous council consisted of some hundred leaders of Israel. According to historic comment, it included the prophets Zechariah, Malachi and Haggai, and several Scribes (Soferim) headed by Ezra and Nehemiah. The "Men of the Great Assembly" formulated a new religious and civil code for the reestablished Jewish settlement in Palestine.

In his volume on Hebrew accentuation, Wickes says: "The notation which fixed the traditional punctuation

---

3 Like many other creators of medieval culture, Saint Gall (550-645), founder of the famous Swiss German monastery, was an Irishman born in Ireland and a disciple of St. Columba, another prominent Irish educator. St. Gall monastery was famous for its school of music, a repository of the ancient church chant.

of each word may well have been introduced at the same period and for the same reasons as the notation which fixed the traditional modulation."

There are reasons to believe that the great Jewish leader and restorer of ancient worship, Ezra the Scribe, not only established the public reading of the Pentateuch and the use of pausal accents—in the fifth century B.C.E.—but also introduced the cantillation. Some writers maintain that Ezra's successors in his educational work, the *Soferim*, the "interpreters," finally fixed the order of cantillation used in the festive reciting of the Bible before the people, as a sort of *seyog la-torah*.

The Talmud remains the best witness to the existence of biblical cantillation during the first centuries C.E., at the latest.

On the authority of Rabbi Iohanan, the tract *Megilla* of the Babylonian Talmud says:

"Who reads the Scriptures without sweetness *(neimo)*, and learns them without a chant *(zimro)*, of him says Prophet Ezekiel: 'And I also have given them laws that are not good.' " [4]

In the Talmudic tracts *Berachot* and *Nedarim*, words of Rabbi Akiba (40-134 C.E.) and the Rav (Abba Areca, one of the great Fathers of the Synagogue who lived in the third century C.E.) also point to the early chanting of the Scriptures. And the all important fact that only those parts of the Scriptures that were read publicly in the days of the Second Temple, possess corresponding chants, confirms further, emphatically so, the age of the traditional cantillation.

[4] Babylonian Talmud. English translation by M. Rodkinson.

Since the earliest times the Hebrew scriptural signs have been marks of grammatical, metrical and logical accents.   But at the same time they serve as specimens of indirect or incomplete musical notation, just as do the early Christian neumes.   The existence of these accents is in itself a telling witness: it presupposes the existence of a corresponding system of cantillation.

The link is so strong that the cantillated biblical verse acquires a metric form tonally correct due to the pausal accents.[5]

One finds precisely the same interrelation within the Christian neumes.

Edmond de Coussemaker, a famed musicologist, was the first definitely to state the origin of the signs and to explain their inner tie with ancient vocalization:

"The neumes have their origin, as we believe, in the accent.   The acute accent, or arsis, the grave accent, or thesis, and the circumflex accent formed by the conjunction of arsis and thesis, are the fundamental signs of all the neumes." [6]

To which Father Gatard adds:

"We have already noticed that the tonic accent has an essentially musical import in Latin, because it indicates a rise of voice.   For this accent to pass on from a grammatical sign to a musical one is but a short step.   As a matter of fact we find the accent-

[5] David Maggid, the Russian scholar, has treated this subject with admirable insight, in his article on biblical cantillation in the *Jewish Encyclopedia* published in Leningrad, and also in his monograph *Ancient Jewish Music and Psalmody* published in the series *De Musica*, issued in 1927 by the State Institute of Art History in Leningrad.

[6] Charles Edmond de Coussemaker: *Histoire de l'harmonie au Moyen Age* (1852).

neumes in all the Eastern liturgies, beginning with
the Byzantine.[7]

* * *

Study of the structure typical of the old Hebrew biblical recitative, has three points of importance:

a) rhythmo-melodic traits;
b) modal features;
c) the degree of structural identity in the chants used
by the various branches of Israel.

The tonal structure of the biblical cantillation is
determined less by its scale-tendencies than by its basic
rhythmo-melodic units, the motives. These correspond
to accents, metric and logical, and have therefore a definite syntactic meaning.

Hebrew accentuation establishes a musical as well as
a grammatical difference between the separating
motives (*mafsikim,* disjunctives) and the binding
motives (*mesharethim,* conjunctives). These motive-
accents, which dominate the building of a musical
phrase, are subdivided. Disjunctives, for example, are
distributed into categories of "kings," "princes,"
"dukes," "counts," etc.; some of them indicate the complete ending of a verse, the full cadence, the others
marking the end of a fractional passage. It is significant
that late medieval polyphonic music has adapted the
titles *dux* and *comes* (duke and count) for the leading
elements of the fugue. Ancient conceptions of the
scriptural chant and late Western forms are thus linked
with an alluring transparency. You will find the sim-

---

[7] Dom Gatard: *Plainchant.* The Faith Press, London.

plest form of the *silluk,* the main disjunctive motive-accent, taken from the notation by Salomo Rosovski of the Hebrew University in Jerusalem (*Table IV, ex.* 1).

A well-known Hebrew Russian composer, now living in Palestine, Salomo Rosovski, has made a considerable research in the cantillation of the Pentateuch according to the Ashkenazic tradition, that of the Jews of Poland, Germany, Russia and the Baltic states. In systematizing that vast ocean of pausal and connecting accents, of signs (*graphemas*) and melodic fragments (*phonemas*) which form the traditional cantillation of the Bible, Rosovski uses a method adapted from biological research.

He selects the musical cell that forms the cadence in each segment of the cantillation, the *silluk,* as a key to a rhythmic analysis of the basic biblical chant. He then follows the modification of the *silluk* from its primitive nucleus, the monosyllable, to words and melodic lines with five and six syllables.

Having analyzed in the same way, musically and grammatically, all the twenty-six *tropes,* that is, all the basic chants and pausal accents of the biblical cantillation, and having compared musical and grammatical evidence gathered by Jewish scholars and musicians, Rosovski has arrived at a formulating of various rules that govern the melodic structure of the biblical chant.

Turning to the modal traits, we find in the cantillation of the Pentateuch and of the Prophets the same modes that are typical also of the later synagogal song, and which I have described earlier, in the chapter "Hebrew Music, Past and Present" of this book. The favorite modes of the Pentateuch and of the Prophets are the Dorian, Phrygian and Hyppodorian of the ancient Greeks, in the Jewish popular terminology, our old acquaintances, the *Adonoy Moloch* and *Mogen Ovos*. They are often modified through a subtle display of motive-combination, a sort of racial tonal caprice.

Joseph Yasser, the well-known New York musicologist, a savant and musician of rare gifts and competence, maintains, however, that the biblical chant has basic and very strong pentatonic traits (*infra-diatonic*, in Yasser's terminology). But his research, too, establishes a structural kinship between the medieval chants of the Catholic Church and the Hebrew cantillation, the source of the former.[8]

It is important to notice that the motives and cadences play an infinitely greater part in the scriptural cantillation, that here they are more intricately used and interwoven, than in the synagogal song of later origin. This is, of course, to be expected as the motives and phrases of the biblical recitative are but a musical vestment of logical and grammatical accents.

The connection with the word and its emphasis is here infinitely closer than in the later sacred melody, with its greater musical freedom.

———

Detail next in importance pertains to the similarity between the chants used by the various branches of the people of Israel.

[8] Bulletin of the New York Musicological Society. November, 1932. Joseph Yasser's opinion in the matter conforms with his remarkable doctrine presented in his *Theory of Evolving Tonality*, published by the American Library of Musicology.

One is impressed by the fact that Jewish tribes far apart, geographically and historically, are using, after centuries of separation, the same modes built of the same motive-details. Only, they do not always apply these chants to the same passages of the Bible. And one sees how clearly the tonal neighborhood of a "new" Jewish settlement, for example, the mid-European major scale, has impressed itself on the old Hebrew modal cantillation. Such, for example, is the case of the biblical recitative that migrated from the Orient to southeastern France or the Rhineland.

I shall take only a few more instances. First, the identity of the Babylonian and the Ashkenazic traditional cantillation of the verses from *Ruth,* or of the Babylonian and Amsterdam Portuguese way of chanting the Pentateuch. David Pinna's notation of the Hebrew Spanish neumes, the basis of the Amsterdam Portuguese cantillation, is published in the introduction of the Bible edited by Daniel Ernest Yablonski for the Markgraf of Brandenburg, in 1699.

The remarkable similarity in the reciting of the Psalms by widely dispersed Jewish communities, also points to a close kinship between numerous traditions within scattered Israel.[9]

* * *

Among the Christian theologians many uphold the traditional antiquity of the Hebrew scriptural cantillation. But at the same time there are Jewish savants such as Eliahu Bachur, who oppose the popular belief.

[9] The second chapter of A. Z. Idelsohn's book on Jewish music abounds in eloquent examples confirming this opinion.

One must note, however, that Eliahu Bachur or Levita, who died in 1549, was influenced in his negation of the antiquity of the Hebrew neumes by his Roman disciple, Cardinal Egidio.[10]

At one time the opinion denying the tradition seemed to have been supported by a document published by the notorious Karaite, Firkovitch. This "document," said to have been found in Dagestan, a region on the Caspian Sea, ascribes the establishing of the accents and punctuation to Rabbi Moshe ha-Nagdan. The eminent orientologist, Dr. Alexander Harkavi, of the St. Petersburg Academy, has proven the document to be a forgery.

Passions and crimes whirling around academic problems, in this case—a serene sacred subject, are indeed curious. But stranger things have happened in the grim past. The great Italian mathematician, Cardano, was said to have killed a colleague during an academic dispute. There also exists a tale of how he forced another great mathematician, Tartaglia, father of the theory of probabilities (a key to the science of insurance), to reveal, at the point of a dagger, an important discovery in higher algebra. Then Cardano published Tartaglia's solution as his own.

Returning to our present controversies, I wish to quote the opinion of David Maggid [11] that "the very

[10] The famous Roman prelate and humanist, Cardinal Egidio (1470-1532), was a friend of the Jewish people and a defender of the Talmud. He addressed to the great Reuchlin the famous words: "Fighting on your behalf, we defend not you but the law, not the Talmud but the Church." See the delectable *A World Passes By,* by Marvin Lowenthal (Harper).

[11] See *Hebrew Cantillation* in the Jewish Encyclopedia, published in Petrograd.

logic and completeness of the musical vocalization of
the Bible, indicates an effort and achievement which
terminates a collective effort of several centuries' dura-
tion." His is an idea forcefully sustained by historical
data, no less than by musical analysis.

Important indirect evidence pointing to the antiquity
of Hebrew cantillation can be obtained from a comparative study of the Hebrew and Christian neumes whose
setting is ascribed to the monk St. Ephrem in the fourth
century C.E.

Many are the facts indicating the common roots of
Hebrew and Christian accentuation.

Their origin is the same—in cheironomy—and their
graphic image is similar. In the earlier mentioned
passage from the Talmudic tract (Berachot 62a) , Rabbi
Akiba and Rabbi Nachman ben Itzchak say: "the hand
is used for leading and showing the meaning of the
text." But the early Christian Church and the ancient
synagogue knew exactly the same kind of cheironomic
gesture of the presbyter. Some scholars interpret one
of the passages from the Gospels (Luke IV, 17) as an
indication that Jesus Christ made cheironomic gestures
while he recited the book on the Prophet Isaiah to the
people.

This is, by the way, another detail confirming the
opinion of distinguished Jewish savants that Jesus of
Nazareth was entirely a Jew, in his breeding as well as
in his predilections and racial allegiance.[12]

12 See Dr. Kaufmann Kohler's *The Origin of the Synagogue and the
Church* (Macmillan) and Dr. H. G. Enelow's *A Jewish View of Jesus*
(Bloch).

The late Dr. H. G. Enelow has shown lucidly that the following can be gathered from the Scriptures:

"Jesus was conscious of his Jewish derivation, as well as of his debt to his Jewish heritage and his duty to the Jewish people. His noblest teachings were illustrated by citations from the Jewish Scriptures, his most solemn admonitions were addressed to the Jewish people, and his most tender words were spoken concerning the Jewish people. 'O Jerusalem, Jerusalem, though thou killest the prophets and stonest them which are sent unto thee, how often would I have gathered thy children together.' "

Still another fact of significance. The Hebrew word *neima* (from *noam*—sweet, pleasing) closely approaches the Greek *neuma*, scriptural sign. Old historical documents reveal kinship between both the verbal image and the metaphors embodied in these twin-words. The link between *neuma* (sign) and *melos* (song) which derives from the Greek *meli*, honey, is telling. Dr. Fleischer remarks justly that the very coupling of a musical sign with the idea of "sweetness," as is done by several ancient races, can be probed profitably by musical science.

It is *à propos* to notice that the kinship of the Hebrew *neima* and the Greek *neuma* is as definitely uniting the mental and racial ancestry of human races as is the kinship of Iou, the ancient Gaelic name of Iona, famous Hebrid island and parish of St. Columba, and the name of Java, of the East Indies, both Iou and Java meaning "corn," *eo-rna* in old Gaelic and Irish.

Finally the Hebrew system of accents—and of corresponding finger-motions and graphic signs, named Tiberian and known since the ninth century c.e.—has a remarkable likeness to the oldest Christian neumes and to the Byzantine and Armenian of early times.[13]

* * *

How then shall one explain this close relation between the old Hebrew and the early Christian cantillation of the Bible: as an historical co-existence of phenomena that spring from the same root, or as an even closer parentage?

This subject is fairly shelled with conflicting dogma.

Arthur Friedlander, a London musician, has offered the following theory: "The converts from Judaism handed down the traditional modes of the cantillation of *the Holy Law* and the *Prophets* (not as has been erroneously supposed, the chants for the Psalms) but in a somewhat corrupted form, subsequently adopting this for the music known as plain-chant." [14]

Some of the learned dignitaries of the Roman Church do not share in the exemption of the psalm-chants from the music that influenced the early Christian vocalization of King David's poems.

Bishop Isidor of Seville, contemporary of Pope Gregory I (sixth century), says: *"Laudes, hoc est Alleluja canere, canticum est Hebraeorum."*—"The

[13] Compare Oscar Fleischer's tables in Chapters VI and VII of Volume I of *Neumen Studien* with the Hebrew accentuation.

[14] Peter Wagner: *Einführung in die Gregorianische Melodien.* Breitkopf and Härtel. Leipzig 1910.

melodies of laudations, that is the chants for the Hallelujah, are Hebrew canticles." [15]

Many centuries later, one of the greatest authorities
on early Christian music, the Benedictine monk, Dom
Joseph Pothier, insisted, in his *Les mélodies grégo-
riennes d'après la tradition,* that with the texts of the
Psalms the ancient church adopted from the Jews not
only the corresponding chants, but even the manner of
distributing the verses between the choir and the
people:

> *"Il n'est guère possible de supposer que l'Eglise
> ait recuélli les paroles sans guarder aucune rémi-
> niscence de la manière dont on s'en servait et des
> mélodies sur lesquelles on les chantait.*
>
> *Quant à l'usage liturgique des Psaumes et des
> Cantiques, c'est-à-dire, au partage du texte et à la
> distribution des rôles entre les choeurs et le peuple,
> nous rémarquons dans la liturgie chrétienne trois
> manières principales, qui etaient également en
> usage dans la liturgie mosaïque."* [16]

* * *

In my earlier days I used to compare the oldest specimens of our biblical cantillation, their graceful,

---

[15] Peter Wagner: *Einführung in die Gregorianische Melodian.* Breitkopf and Härtel. Leipzig 1910.

[16] "It is not possible to suppose that the Church has recorded the
texts without having preserved any reminiscence of the manner in
which these words were used, and of the melodies with which the
latter were sung. As to the liturgical use of the Psalms and of the
Canticles, that is, as to the division of the text and the distribution of
the rôle between the choir and the congregation, we notice in the
Christian liturgy the same three principal manners that were in use
of the Mosaic liturgy." Dom Joseph Pothier: *Les melodies grégo-
riennes d'après la tradition.* Tournai, 1879.

capricious and developed embroidery with such rugged, straight-lined ancient church contemporaries as the traditional Ambrosian *Beatus vir* (Psalm I) and *Kyrie* of Tutillo, or *Media vita in morte* of Notker Balbulus[17] or the hymn *A solis ortu* composed for the funeral of Charlemagne.[18] With much youthful and nationalist ardor and a rather slight armament of facts, I then maintained that the Ambrosian chant was a rough and hardened, an underdeveloped issue of the ancient Hebrew chant.[19]

However, competent historians have expressed opinions that indorse some points of my old belief.

In the chapter on Psalms and Psalmody of his *Einführung in die Gregorianischen Melodien,* Peter Wagner insists that even the later part of the early Christian era used only a primitive form of church-recitative. *"Eine Stelle in den Konfessionen des heiliges Augustinus wird meist hervorgezogen, um die Meinung zu bekräftigen das noch über das IV Jahrhundert hinaus reichere melodische Formen dem Kirchengesang fremd gewesen seien."* [20]

This fact serves as indirect evidence of the Hebrew parentage of the plain-chant, a dogma upheld categorically by Christian savants.[21] It is clear that fanatical

---

[17] August Wilhelm Ambros: *Geschichte der Musik,* chapter on Byzantium. F. E. C. Leuckart, Leipzig.

[18] Emil Naumann: *Illustrierte Musikgeschichte.*

[19] L. Saminsky: *Hebrew Music.* Petrograd, 1914.

[20] "A Passage in the Confessions of St. Augustine is usually quoted to confirm the opinion that up to an epoch as late as the fourth century c.e., the richer melodic forms of the church-song were foreign."

[21] It is à *propos* to mention here an interesting thought of Arthur Mendel, the gifted young New York writer on music: "Was Gregorian

early Christian creed forbade any interference with the ecclesiastical recitative, a revered part of the Old Testament tradition. In some of the ultra-conservative cloisters the primitive canticle was preserved intact up to the late Middle Ages.

But then, of course, a Jewish writer would come forth to deny any genetic connection between ancient Hebrew and Christian music.

Thus writes Rabbi Francis L. Cohen:

"No Hebrews could have preserved either the ancient Templar style, or the melodies built upon it, if the system adopted by the Catholic Church had really exhibited such ancient Israelitish paternity as is claimed for it. Nor could the Jewish music, in employing similar scales to those afterwards known as Ambrosian and Gregorian, have been influenced by the church tones, because quite apart from the possession of similar tonality by the more ancient scriptural cantillation, we know very well that the most famous of the early arrangers and supporters of the Catholic psalmody and hymnody were merciless foes of the Jews. The famous Ambrose, Bishop of Milan in the fourth century, distinguished himself by his intemperate harshness against the Synagogue no less than by his arrangement of the Christian service of song. We can scarcely imagine that he, or others, would have consented to 'Judaize' the church music, or that the Jews would have imitated the tones used in the worship of men who destroyed their homes and

chant Western music? Spengler would say, 'No.' It flowered before the beginning of Western culture (900-1000 c.e.), and its decay was simultaneous with the growth of Western music." Arthur Mendel: *Spengler and Music History*, "Musical Quarterly," April 1934.

burnt their synagogues under the plea of religion." [22]

This argument is in the same half-scientific, half-artistic vein as is Renan's famous proof of the non-existence of Moses or his repudiation of the Exodus.

Rabbi Cohen's purely psychological casuistics, drowning in a torrent of dramatic verbiage, are in contradiction to every bit of historical evidence. The facts enumerated in the chapter "Hebrew Music, Past and Present" in this book, as well as those listed in the present essay, clearly prove that no racial dislike or religious controversy has ever hindered musical interchange. No hatred has ever barred the annexing of a neighbor's tune. The neighbor is damned or burned, the tune christened and taken into the family. This is one of the blessings of art which not the fiercest creed will contravene.

In a much more ferocious and fanatical time, at the very height of the Crusades with their savage extermination of the Jews, none other than the famous prelate and chancellor of the University of Paris, known by the inelegant name of Pierre le Mangeur or Petrus Comestor (Peter the Glutton, who died in 1179), wove into his *Historia Scholastica* a number of rabbinical tales and commentaries. This book had a tremendous vogue, and it influenced the Christian preaching and the secular European literature for generations.

If an eminent Christian divine and educator of the Dark Ages thought nothing of utilizing rabbinical tales,

[22] From the lectures of Rabbi Francis L. Cohen, quoted by A. Friedlander.

why is it impossible that some of the Christian musicians should have adapted Hebrew chants?

However, another Hebrew writer, D. A. de Sola, parries Rabbi Cohen's argument in his own way. In his *Ancient Melodies of Spanish and Portuguese Jews* he insists that the chanting of the first Christians derived from the Hebrew temple-song and should therefore be linked to the chanting of the levites, to the musical usages of Ezra Hassofer and to the Hebrew cantillation of the first centuries of Christianity. He asks very convincingly:

"Is not all the historic evidence sufficient to convince us that the Apostles, who were born Hebrews, brought up in the customs of their nation, who frequented the Temple and engaged in prayers and divine praises therein recited, should retain the same method and use the same chants with which the people used to respond to the levitical choir?

"We may remark in addition, that it is quite improbable that the early Christians should have adopted melodies used by idolaters for the purpose of idolatry. Not only was this prohibited to them by the teachers (See Forkel's *Geschichte der Musik*), but they were themselves naturally averse to adopt them. Thus Clement of Alexandria, who flourished in the third century, would allow the guitar and lyre to be used at social festivities—because David played on them—but prohibited the flute—because that instrument was used in the service of idolatry. They therefore could not use any other than the old Hebrew melodies with which they were acquainted from early habit and association."

We shall see further that the latest research and the most solid Christian authorities support this plausible view without hesitation.

A. Friedlander endorses de Sola's opinion by a discovery, among other things, that the famous *Te Deum Laudamus* of St. Ambrose startlingly resembles the chant used by the Jewish people for ages when reciting a passage from the Prophet Zechariah: *Roni v'simchi bas Zion* (Rejoice, ye daughter of Zion). And he emphasizes the fact that a number of great medieval church-musicians were of Hebrew origin; Guido d'Arezzo himself was said to be of Jewish descent.

It is indeed very startling to learn that the monk, J. Boeschenstein (1472-1540), who explained to the great humanist, Joseph Reuchlin, the musical meaning of the accentuation of the Pentateuch, was not only a friend and disciple of various Jewish scholars but was himself of Jewish descent.

The notation prepared by Boeschenstein was published in Reuchlin's *De Accentibus et Orthographia Hebraeorum.*[23]

But the most illuminating fact is that a great modal similarity exists between the Hebrew Oriental version of the Pentateuch and one of the basic Gregorian modes; and this mode is used by those very communities whose rites and musical tradition clearly originated in the early Babylonian Jewish settlements, which had no link with the Roman church. This is why the extraordinary

[23] Copies of Reuchlin's book published in Hagenau in 1518 can be seen in the New York Library and at the Hebrew Union College in Cincinnati. Prof. Idelsohn reproduces a fragment of Reuchlin's notation in his book on Jewish music.

melodic sameness of several ancient synagogal tunes handed down to us from the Jews of southern France, Italy and the Rhineland, with some of the famous medieval chants, should by no means be construed as evidence that the Jews borrowed their sacred melodies from the Christian church.

———————

This *exposé* is not guided by any scientific pretension. I neither attempt to present complete data on the sub- ject, nor do I wish to rush into combat with learned men who have consumed a lifetime in this study.

My limited aim is to present a clear vision of the twisted old stream of biblical chanting, to make its more important curves and angles transparent. But even this end cannot be achieved without delving to the bedrock of the evidence.

Let us scrutinize still more closely the facts concern- ing the dawn of the Hebrew scriptural melos and also the latter's tangible link with the early Christian plain- chant. This time, however, I prefer to take the age of the ancient church melos as a lever for the discussion, rather than again to sift the antiquity of the Hebrew chant.

Authorities on early Christian music state that the Ambrosian hymns were *"responsorials et antiphonals,"*[24] just as was the ancient Hebrew music.

In his excellent book on plain-chant, Father Gatard insists that the data on the Roman chant used since

———

[24] Dom Ambroise Kienle: *Théorie et partique du chant Grégorien,* Tournai, 1888.

time immemorial and discovered in manuscripts of the ninth century, reveal a perfect, not an embryonic state of the Roman plainsong. Father Gatard shows that specimens of this chant spread all over civilized continental Europe by orders of the Carolingian kings, were only codified by Pope Gregory the Great (540-604) ; that neither St. Gregory, nor the later occupants of St. Peter's throne added to those beautiful ancient canticles or composed new ones.[25]

John the Deacon, contemporary and biographer of St. Gregory, states categorically:

"This great Pope, most zealous of singers, compiled an Antiphonary collection which is of the greatest value. Also he founded the song-school (*Schola cantorum*) which still sings in the Roman Church the chant that bears his name. At the *Schola*,[26] the couch on which he lay when singing, the rod with which he threatened the boy-choristers, and the original Antiphonary are preserved."

St. Gregory sent copies of his antiphoner, with singers, to teach people how to recite them, to various courts, among these to Theodolind, wife of Autaris, King of the Langobards (Lombards) , and a gentleman belonging to that imaginative family who made skulls of their enemies into drinking mugs. Theodolind's antiphoner adorned with gold and silver letters may still be seen in the cathedral of Monza, near Milan.

One of the heirs to St. Gregory, Pope Paul, had an

25 Dom Gatard: *Plain Chant*. Faith Press, London 1921.
26 That is, at the ancient Palace of Lateran which does not now exist.

antiphoner sent to Pepin the Short; and Pope Adrian I delegated, at the request of Charlemagne, some of his monk-choirmasters to establish schools of plain-chant singing in Metz and Soissons.

St. Gregory's work of codification and compilation seems to have consisted only in *"multa substrahens, pauca convertens, nonnulla vero superadicens,"* that is, in "eliminating much, altering little, adding something." Dom Gatard points to "the striking similarity between the Ambrosian and Gregorian chants; their common ancestry . . . the former chant being like a thick forest filled with luxuriant growth, the latter like a planned park . . ." and adds: "We naturally associate the tunes used for these hymns, psalms, and songs with those used in the Temple at Jerusalem, or in the synagogues of the Diaspora." [27]

Now, if no substantial alteration in the *used* hymns occurred—and apparently it did not—from the opening of the Ambrosian epoch up to the close of the Gregorian, why should there have been musical changes during the period that stretches between the destruction of the Second Temple and the age of St. Ambrose? If it is true that the Hebrew scriptural chant was sacred to the first Christians, then the continuity of biblical cantillation through the two thousand years seems irrefutable.

But there can be not the slightest doubt as to an interweaving of the old Christian tradition with the old Hebrew usage.

Hieronymus (St. Jerome), editor of the *Vulgata,* the Latin Bible, lived in Palestine between 386 and 420 C.E.,

[27] Dom Gatard, *ibidem.*

and he takes pride in the fact that his translation is an issue from the purest Hebrew sources.

If the ancient Roman church attributed such importance to the authenticity of the Hebrew literary text, it is clear that the church could not be other than just as strict as to the sanctity of the Hebrew musical tradition.

Facts pertaining to the ancient chants used in reciting the Lament of Jeremiah sustain this reasoning forcefully.

Dr. Fleischer quotes a version of the Lament which he considers the oldest; its modal structure is exactly the same as that of the primordial Hindu and Greek sacred hymns.[28]   This traditional cantillation of the Lament is the one listed in *Officium majoris hebdomadae,* the official collection of the oldest traditional songs of the Roman church; and it is sung now in exactly the same manner as it was sung in the time of the Amiatine Bible.[29]

Also, of the Old Scriptures, the Lament was the first book supplied with the oldest type of Latin neumes. This fact as well as the circumstances of Hieronymus' work on the *Vulgata,* speak most eloquently of both the age and the kinship of the Hebrew and Christian cantillation.

Fleischer's argument is as lucid as it is invulnerable.

"Die Klagelieder Jeremia lernten die Christen um so leichter, als sie sich anfangs in ähnlicher Lage wie die Juden befanden und sich auch sonst

[28] Oscar Fleischer: *Neumen Studien,* Vol. II, Chapter II.

[29] *Codex Amiatinus,* English copy of the *Vulgata,* St. Hieronymus' Latin version of the Bible, was made by order of the Northumbrian Bishop Ceolfrid and presented to Pope Gregory II in 716.

*gar mancher Rest alter jüdischer Gebräuche in der
Christlichen Liturgie erhalten hat . . . Denn whol
gemerkt: es war nich eine Melodie, ein melo-
disches Einzelgebilde, was diese Klagelieder auf-
weisen, sondern eine musikalische Form, eine
Recitations-Formel, ein Deklamations-Schema."* [30]

It is very interesting to know that the historical continuity of the chant of Jeremiah was enhanced in St.
Gregory's time by its use as a general elegy and as a
lament for the deceased in later time.

Fleischer remarks very rightly that neither have the
Jewish people forgotten these chants originally created
by themselves. He points to the well-known synagogal
collections of A. Eisenstadt, cantor of the Berlin community and to Samuel Naumburg's *Chants religieux
israélites.* I would add to this a striking fact. A traditional synagogal psalm, known as the *Lamnatzeach*
of Zeidl Rovner (a cantor revered by the orthodox
Jewry), is almost a replica of the aboriginal *Lament* of
Jeremiah sacred to the Roman Church since antiquity.

I have used this characteristic *Lamnatzeach* chant in
my biblical ballet *Rachel,*[31] to depict the aggrieved
Leah, the elder daughter of Laban, rejected by the patri-
arch Jacob for the sake of the younger, Rachel.

* * *

[30] "The Christians adopted the chants for 'Jeremiah's Lament' the
easier that at the beginning they found themselves in a similar position,
that is, victims of persecution as were the Jews; much of the rest of
the old Hebrew usages was preserved in the Christian liturgy. . . .
For it is clear: these lamentations point not to a melody, to a single
melodic image, but to a musical form, a recitation-formula, a scheme
for musical declamation."

[31] Lazare Saminsky: *Lamentation de Rachel.* Editions Maurice
Senart, Paris.

Then, to sum up the interminable discussion on the music of the Bible, it is safe to consider the following thesis concrete and impregnable.

The ancient and the new musician, be it the early medieval Bishop Isidore of Seville, or the modern Jewish musicologist, the Protestant savant Saalschütz [32] or the Catholic scholar, Father Gatard, all unite in one belief. They maintain that the Ambrosian era adapted and ingrained into the church-ritual, the popular Oriental song that originated in the chants of the Temple levites.   To make this union of savants of various creeds and of conflicting types of erudition perfect, new discoveries of some Eastern papyri bring out another important point.   The vocalization in the ancient Hebrew chanting had its unmistakable counterpart in the ornate early Christian scriptural recitative.

In the distinct chain of continuity—from the chanting of *Shema Israel*, "Hear, O Israel" in the Temple of Solomon to the plain-song recited today at the Capella Julia of St. Peter's in Rome—some very recent links are known.   A new impetus was given this ancient melos by the famous encyclical *Motu Proprio* of Pope Pius X who, at the beginning of this century, ordered a rigid reintroduction of the ancient Gregorian canticle into the Roman ritual.   Similar work has been accomplished by the later Jewish composers for the synagogue.   The restoration of the fine old Byzantine neume-chants to the Russian Orthodox Church was achieved by Alexander Kastalsky, an outstanding Russian musician.

[32] The author of *Geschichte und Würdigung der Musik bei den Hebräern.*

One may, however, seek after and guess at a still older font of the ancient biblical canticle, both Jewish and Christian.

In my early book on Hebrew music I indicated the strangely antivocal structure of some of the oldest biblical chants, their wind-instrumental traits. I there express a hypothesis favorably commented on, that these chants may have derived from the fanfares of the primeval wood wind instruments used in the ancient Temple, whose notes are steps of the natural scale. Following the melodic curves of such ancient fragments of our biblical cantillation as the trop *Bateiro,* the basic chant of the Pentateuch *(Table IV, ex. 2)* or the *Oz yoshir Moshe,* "Thus sang Moses" *(Table IV, ex. 3),* in use by the centuries-old community of Carpentras, in Southern France (an issue of the old Babylonian chant), one perceives there a strong outline of the natural scale. All the sustained tones, the corner stones of these melodic formations, are nothing but the clear basic sounds of the natural scale. The short passing notes correspond to the similar sounds of the natural scale; they are marked by the typical vagueness of intonation that our ear, attuned to the tempered scale, perceives as false, out of tune.

In some of the traditional synagogal songs that have felt the influence of the oldest biblical cantillation, one finds the same telling detail of melo-form, the same short passing sounds of a shaky intonation, the same structural tendency of a brass-fanfare.

* * *

This is a joyous vista: the vision of our ancient chants as roots of the Hebrew tonal past and trunk of our tonal future.   Some even share in the happy belief that the traditional Hebrew recitative and the old biblical chant form the sole ground for a renaissance of the grand old Hebrew musical art.   To these believers, the light so definitely turned on the path to the restoring of the ancient music of the biblical era, is heartening indeed.

Let us not, however, give vent here, as in similar cases, to the vain feeling that it was our people who set the tonal roots, out of which grew the great church music of the Christian West.

There is nothing to be proud of.   Let us humbly recall *what* Western art has grown out of the seeds, the ancient Hebrew melos.   Out of these spores divine tonal foliage has sprung: the music of Orlando di Lasso and of other great Netherlanders, the art of Palestrina and Sebastian Bach.   One thinks wistfully of that sublime fragment of biblical poetry, Psalm XLII, which Palestrina rekindled in one of the greatest pages of music ever conceived.   This noble poem moved our own Mendelssohn to nothing more than stereotyped tonal formalities.

For Jewish cultured music, as such, the colossal epoch of the Middle Ages and of the New Era is one interminable desert, a vacuum.   Our musician still stands before his magnificent tonal heritage, with no inkling of how to cultivate it.

But as long as our enchanted ear still listens, at least, in a remote Orthodox synagogue, to the beautiful melodic thread of *Vayih bime Achashverosh* (And it came to pass, in the days of king Ahasuerus) or the *Shir hashirim asher li-Shelomo* (the Song of Songs of King Solomon), chants carried by the Jewish people through the ages, all nations, all countries, we are still watching the biblical chant—a living, creating force, such as is and will remain to be the Bible itself.

By birthright it is the task of the Hebrew musician to transfuse these gentle brooks of adorable old melos, preserved by a miracle, into cultured art, to sustain the immortality of our ancient canticle. But while a Jewish task primarily, the fostering of this biblical melody should be just as precious to the Universal Forum.

PART VII

JEWISH FOLKSONG, ORIGINAL OR
BORROWED?

JEWISH FOLKSONG, ORIGINAL
OR BORROWED?

FACTS AND POLEMIC

In his admirable essay, "A Discussion of Banality," the well-known American writer, Oscar Thompson, has stated very lucidly the case of hasty recognition granted to pseudo-folklore.

> "There is the possibility that a rhythmic or melodic pattern, commonplace enough in its habitat, but tardy in getting abroad, may escape at the outset the tag of banality that would have been fastened on it if it had been the everyday story elsewhere that it was at home." [1]

The very newness of Hebrew folksong, the lateness of its emergence in the West is responsible for a false understanding of the true Hebraic melodic type.

In January, 1915 I had published, in the Petrograd weekly *Razsviét* ("The Dawn") an article entitled "Recent Works of the Hebrew Folksong Society" in which I accused the previous works of having banal musical foundation. This evoked a spirited letter to the press from Julius Engel, the famous Moscow critic and father of Jewish folksong collecting in Russia. Our polemic raged, in the press and at public gatherings,

[1] Oscar Thompson: *Practical Musical Criticism,* Witmark Publications, New York 1934.

from 1915 to 1923, with various interested bystanders and professionals, Russian, German and French, participating. This controversy stirred up the matter very thoroughly, and has contributed material which illumines the dark domain of Jewish folksong with advantage to musical science. My youthful nationalist ardor pitched this battle of ideas, but it was humanized by entertaining and humorous repartee. I find it useful to reproduce my initial article that started the controversy, and also the summary of my opponents' replies followed by my further epistles *in extenso*.

RECENT WORKS OF THE HEBREW FOLKSONG SOCIETY

The Hebrew Folksong Society in Petrograd has now ended a five years' work of research and cultivation of true specimens of Hebrew music. One notices an important change in the work's direction. I mean a shifting of interest from the domestic folksong, which engaged the initial labors of the Society's composers, to the religious folksong, to its pure and ancient elements.

During the first years of the Hebrew Folksong Society its workers recorded almost solely the domestic tunes or the semi-religious chassidic songs with similar musical traits. A number of assimilated songs, clearly borrowed from Oriental music, from Polish folk-dances, etc., were collected with gusto. This motley collection included very odd shipmates adopted with a naïve belief in the sanctity of everything that our people sings. Thus a metamorphosis of a Ukrainian song *Hob ich a por oksen* (I have a yoke of oxen), a typically German song *Schön bin ich, schön,*[2] a travesty of *badchon* couplets [3] *Der Philosoph,* and an anonymous mediocre cantorial song written to an electrifying melodramatic text *Eili, Eili,* were very piously given shelter as Jewish folksongs.

Those first works of the Hebrew Folksong Society do not even touch the rich mine of our religious melody of the ancient type, with its creative potentialities and value to musical science.

The blunder was, of course, only too natural in those first years of indiscriminate enthusiasm for the vista of national musical art just opened up. But the growth of a theoretical analysis of Hebrew music and a critical attitude of our composers toward their own work, toward its *national-artistic* side, have driven our young writers into the realm of the truest and noblest elements of Jewish music. At last, a tangible result in both domains, the recording of folksongs and composition based on the latter, is achieved.

The latest extensive collection of Hebrew songs in Southern Russia, Volynia, Lithuania, Palestine and Georgia, mainly records the purest type of the religious melody in use by our people. In the new compositions published by the Society, one notices the same displacement of tendency from domestic toward religious music.

The bulk of these works are by the most gifted among the member-composers: the violin pieces by Achron

[2] See the *Collection of Jewish Folksongs* published by the Petrograd Society.

[3] *Badchon* is a Jewish minstrel, a very popular figure in the old Jewish ménage, especially at weddings.

and Gniéssin, the vocal pieces and choral *Unsane Tokef* by Milner, the Chassidic trio by Rosovski and songs by Lioubóv Streicher. Of these compositions, only Achron's pieces (his delectable *Hebrew Melody,* for instance), broad and individual as is their manner of treating the folksong, still gravitate to the proceeding and spirit of the domestic folksong.

On the contrary, the clear-sighted Rosovski and the highly gifted Milner enlarge their form significantly; their way of cultivating the elements of the religious folksong marks a new, important and fruitful change of direction in the latest Jewish composition.

Milner's beautiful *In Heider* and also his splendid choral *Unsane Tokef* pour into Hebrew art a stream of accent, melodic turn and intonation sheltered before only in the original traditional melos of our old *shul* (synagogue) and our old *cheder* (religious school). Rosovski's *Trio* welds interestingly the developing of a domestic melody—a dance song of the Lithuanian *chassidim*—with the ornamental curve flowing from the traditional synagogal recitative.

The same spirit imbues the smaller pieces of the series, the fine violin air *Nigun von Shǎike Pfaifer* (The Melody of Isaiah the Whistler) by Michael Gniéssin, the lovely *Song of Songs* by the highly talented Lioubóv Streicher and the cello piece of Léon Zeitlin, *Eli Zion,* where most skillfully the fine traditional chant for King Solomon's *Song of Songs* is introduced as a *coda.*

Thus one notices in the newest work of the young Hebrew composers a fresh current. They tend to enlarge their form, on the one hand, and on the other, to put to a more extensive use the proceedings of our religious music, the most characteristic and stately elements of Jewish folk-art.

In my opinion, this points to a new goal for Hebrew music. One may feel sure that the birth of the largest form which would sum up and crown the Jewish tonal thought is not far off. I mean the birth of Jewish national opera.

The appearance of such opera will be a dazzling manifestation of a renaissance of our ancient grand musical art. It will cause all dispersed rivulets of Hebrew composition to converge into one great stream.

————

This article evoked an energetic attack from Julius Engel, in the form of a letter to the press. He took me to task particularly for denying musical value to the chassidic song, which, it will be perceived, I had not done. His epistle was full of lofty feeling but not particularly convincing. "It is rare to find a crusader in a big cause whose intellect is as strong as his battle ax"—to use the brilliant epigram of Nicolas Slonimsky.[4] My answer, a letter to the press, runs as follows.

————

THE VALUE OF JEWISH DOMESTIC MELODY

(A reply to Julius Engel)

In your recent open letter you challenged my argument maintaining that the national value of Jewish

————

[4] Nicolas Slonimsky's article on that indomitable explorer, Henry Cowell, published in *American Composers on American Music*. Stanford University Press.

domestic song and of the similar chassidic melody, is problematic, as this music bears a fatal imprint of alien influence, that of Oriental music, of the Polish folk-dance, etc. You also challenge my conviction of the primacy of our old traditional sacred melos, a superiority flowing from its racial purity.

Having expressed surprise at my "light dismissal of the musical value of the chassidic melody," you end your letter in this way:

> "But . . . you should be only too well aware of my reasons: you yourself are a keen and true worker in the difficult and virgin domain of Hebrew music, an explorer of long standing! How then should one explain your cruel verdict condemning the Jewish domestic song, even the chassidic religious melody? There must be some misunderstanding about it. . . ."

But there is no misunderstanding whatever in my argument. My opinion in the matter was formulated earlier and substantiated. In the first collection of my essays on Hebrew music [5] published as early as 1914, I stated categorically that the new Jewish musician shifts his interest from the trite Oriental type of the domestic song to the elevated type of religious melody, and that the value, high or nil, of Hebrew tonal creation depends on which of these patterns is taken as a basis. [6]

I agree that so sweeping an assertion must be backed by extensive melodic material and by a thorough anal-

---

[5] Lazare Saminsky: *Hebrew Music* published in Petrograd, 1914.

[6] In the opening essay of this book, *The Song of Zion in Exile,* this opinion is quoted more fully.

ysis. I am preparing such an analysis now. Much as I dislike to pluck out single details of a systematic work, I am compelled to do so.

First, your reproach of my "light dismissal of the *musical value* of the religious chassidic melody" has no ground. I spoke only of the *national value* of chassidic melody. This is clear from both the general import of my article and from its following passage: "The growth of a theoretical analysis of Hebrew music, the critical attitude of our composers toward the *national-artistic* side of their own work, have yielded tangible results. . . ."

I beg to say that it was not casual, my rating of some of the folksongs used by our composers, as being doubtful in regard to their national value. I mean such songs as *Hob ich a por Oksen,* of Ukrainian origin, or *Schön binn Ich, schön,* of manifest German descent. These melodies have been treated as having a *national*-Jewish value, have been arranged into compositions and even grace an important Jewish folksong collection published for use in schools and the home.

You ask: where is the folksong free from alien accretion? You point out that even in the synagogue "one hears melodies borrowed from well known operas, but that this does not disqualify the real pearls of traditional synagogal music." You say that "one must be able to tell wheat from chaff."

True enough! The fact in this case, however, is that alien accretion has never managed to fasten itself on the sturdy trunk of our traditional synagogal melody. To segregate the borrowed element and to eliminate it, presents no difficulty. It is certainly impossible to confuse a fragment of the biblical cantillation, the *Shir hashirim,* for instance, or that creation of synagogal genius, *Hayom haras olam* of Nissié Beldzer, with an opera air that has blundered into the synagogue. One could not confuse these true utterances of Hebrew melodic genius with specimens of even our assimilated art, such as a well rounded synagogal air of Sulzer or Naumburg, an imitation of the Catholic and Lutheran church chant. Matters are quite different with the Jewish domestic song. Even its specimens musically valuable present such a knot of alien influences, that the crystallizing of the purest examples is most difficult.

I shall show further that it is just the favorite, just the cherished, the seemingly *our very own* melodies— the chassidic song, among them—that are the most liable to lead us into the error of attributing to them a national or a racial significance.

In these chassidic chants—and in the domestic song as well—there are two interacting mediums. Only a definite segregation of each makes, in my opinion, true appraisal of the national-creative value possible. The general spirit, the psychological subsoil and the verbal substance of the chassidic air must be considered independently of the purely musical structure.

That particular racial enthusiasm which these songs evoke is caused mainly by their general spirit. A dribbling of musical Jewishness as seen in the *Kaddish* of Rabbi Levi Itzhak, for instance,[7] is of much lesser

---

[7] See the description and full text of this *Kaddish* in the essay *Hebrew Music, Past and Present* in this book.

account.   But the majority of the chassidic *nigunim*
—mainly those from Lithuania and Volynia (Western
Ukraine) —bear a trite Oriental modal imprint.   Rhyth-
mically, they are patterned after the Polish folk-dance
—take the *Redl* of the Rabbi of Liubavitch,[8] for
example—or after the Roumanian folksong.   A specimen of the latter is the famous *Volochl,* also of Liubavitch origin; it has been arranged into a lovely piece for
violin by Pavel Lvov, one of the most gifted and
masterly men of the Hebrew Folksong Society constellation.   Some of these *nigunim,* such as the
Makarover nigun or *A redl wie men singt sie* [9] are so
muddy as to their ingredients, and so indistinct racially
that one can see no reason for including them in a Jewish folksong collection.

A propòs, let us take particular notice of the source
of the very stubborn · *eidolon fori* [10] maintaining that
Jewish music as such does not really exist, that it is
but a slightly modified common Oriental melos.   Pop-
ularity and melodic triteness of the well-known Oriental
kind, a mark of so many domestic and chassidic tunes,
support this banal mass-view.

Let us juxtapose two religious folksongs: one specimen of the common Oriental chassidic kind, say, this
very *Kaddish* of Rabbi Levi Itzhak, and one of our
grand and original old synagogal recitatives, the en-

---

[8] A charming roundel formerly sung and danced by the chassidim
adherents of this famous Lithuanian saint.   See No. 61 of the *Sammelbuch,* the folksong collection published by the Hebrew Folksong Society,
Petrograd.

[9] *Ibidem.*

[10] Common prejudice, in Francis Bacon's terminology.

chanting *Omar Rabbi Eliozor* gathered at an old Lithuanian shrine.[11] The first impresses one mightily; it evokes a potent national or racial emotion. The cause of this reaction lies, however, in the general and dramatic substance of this song, in its psychological subsoil, in the racial appeal, in its peculiar and powerful wording, in everything but *musical*-national or *musical*-racial substance.

One finds just the reverse in the epic *Omar Rabbi Eliosor.* A lightning effect as in the *Kaddish* is not produced, but the chant is an infinitely more precious, a most beautiful specimen of the true, racial Hebrew melos. Here flows the characteristic and fragrant wave of our old religious chant, marked by its traditional modal bend and its epic expression. From the same source come wonderful examples of Jewish personal composition such as the sacred melodies created by the genius of Nissan Beldzer, *Hayom haras olam* and *T'ka b'shofar gadol,* and the rarest domestic songs of the elevated type, the exquisite lullaby *Sh'chav sh'chav, bni* ascribed to the saintly "Alter Rov" (the Old Rabbi, that is, the great Schneur Zalmon), for example.

Therefore, one must conclude that the typical chassidic *nigunim* with their non-distinctive, trite and common Oriental structure, cannot be expected to germinate stable musical form of racial nature and of lasting value. A composer caught in the lively stream of Jewish folk-art may, of course, be lured by any musi-

---

[11] Published with my harmonization by the Petrograd Folksong Society; also reproduced in my book *Music of Our Day,* in the chapter on Russian-Oriental Music.

cal and psychological element of the folksong. This is, after all, the manner in which personal creation built on folk-art, begins.

But the one who has set out to seek the original and genuine, the sole and true basis of renascent Hebrew music, must fight this lure, must combat even his own taste and affection. He must discard pitilessly everything doubtful, everything alien.

———

After this letter Mr. Engel was silent for about a year. But apparently the sting of a lost cause did not give its paladin any rest. He came out again with a more substantial criticism of my points and backed it with a profusion of detail. His argument will be quite clear from my answer which follows.

———

STILL MORE ON DOMESTIC SONG
(A reply to Julius Engel)

In Mr. Engel's recent repartee I must call attention first to his error in stretching the meaning and the breadth of my statements too widely. Mr. Engel speaks constantly of my "negation of the Jewish extra-synagogal folksong," while I continually underline the racial-artistic value of not only the sacred Hebrew melos but also of the highest types of domestic folk-music, difficult to extricate from the general flow.

The gist of my argument is clearly this. Hebrew art should cultivate the old sacred chant, which is—Mr. Engel himself is forced to confess—the "basic material" of Jewish folk-music. But withal one should search for and foster the highest, the truly national melodic type of our domestic song, such as the already mentioned *Old Rabbi's Lullaby.*

We should abandon the doubtful guiding rod of the banal and trite type of our domestic and chassidic music, a medium doubtful as to both its aesthetic worth and its racial purity.

But, after all, my own practices refute the incriminating against me of a flat denial of the extra-synagogal folksong's worth. As a composer I have never ceased cultivating the folksong. Thus both theoretically and practically, I recognize, respond emotionally to the beauty of our domestic folk-air.

The question is only: which?

Owing to the same error, the stretching of the meaning and aim of my argument, Mr. Engel unduly inflates also the scope of my forecast when he quotes me in this manner:

> "The Jewish domestic melody and the chassidic *nigunim* cannot become germs of musical-national organisms."

But . . . in my initial note that touched off this controversy, ("Recent Works of the Hebrew Folksong Society") , I speak of the chassidic melodies *only,* I even limit them to the "typical ones," that is, to the ordinary and banal. For even in that *exposé* I did not lose sight of the highest, most valuable type, such as the enchanting chassidic song taken by Moussorgski for his cantata *Joshua, the Son of Nun.*

When I said "the typical chassidic *nigunim* with their characterless, banal Oriental structure cannot germinate national art-organisms," I naturally meant by "typical" the melodies *considered* or recognized by the common belief as typical, used as such.

A reservation concerning the "typical" chassidic *nigunim* had the same aim as my persistent segregating of the highest, the nationally valuable type of domestic melody. This reservation was made with the very hope of insuring my statement from a too broad and an erroneous interpretation.

It is clear then that my debate with Mr. Engel should simmer down to a concrete problem. Of the chassidic and domestic songs, which should be considered the most valuable, as to their national-artistic traits?

Our controversy must then enter into a comparative appraisal of the various kinds of our folksong. And I beg you to notice that the thing I shall always speak of, is the common and popular kind of domestic and chassidic melody marked by the ordinary Oriental traits, the kind I frankly dislike.

* * *

In my opinion, Mr. Engel's most effective criticism is that directed against my argument concerned with the lack of rhythmic originality in the chassidic *nigunim*, which he finds in my following words:

> "The majority of the chassidic *nigunim*— mainly from Lithuania and Volynia (Western Ukraine) —bear a trite Oriental modal imprint. Rhythmically, they are patterned after the Polish

folk-dances, the *Redl* of the Rabbi from Liubavitch, for instance, or after the Roumanian folksongs, the famous *Volochl,* for example, which is
also of Liubavitch origin, etc. In some of these
nigunim the ingredients are so muddy, so indistinct
racially that one can see no reason for including
them in a Jewish folk-song collection."

Mr. Engel attacks particularly my statement regard-
ing the "overwhelming" influence of the alien song on
the very structure of our chassidic melody. He tries
to prove, by one song after another, that it is impossible
to speak of the overwhelming influence of the Polish
dance and of the Ukrainian song. I find, however,
among influences not only the Polish and Ukrainian
tunes, but also the Hungarian, the Bulgar varieties of
the Turkoman songs, and so on.

It may be idle to qualify the Polish or Ukrainian
influence as "prevalent" or "overwhelming." But after
some resistance, even Mr. Engel is compelled to admit
the Ukrainian imprint, which, let us note, is grafted
on the *nigunim* less than any other alien growth. One
is forced, however, to grant a strong influence from
the non-Jewish neighbors. My word substantiating it
is that of a musician who has gathered hundreds of
folksongs and numerous others with a Polish, Lithuanian, Hungarian, Roumanian, Bulgarian (in the South-
Russian districts), Turko-Tartar stamp. Should I not
be given credence when I sum up this grand total and
state that there is an overwhelming non-originality
in the domestic and chassidic song? I may add also
that having been born in a small Russian-Roumanian

village near Odessa, having visited constantly that
neighborhood, an extraordinary crossroad of races,
with thick clusters of Moldavans (Russian Roumanians) , Jews, Ukrainians, Poles, even Bulgars,—I know
very well whence come these numerous chassidic tunes,
love songs and wedding dances, whence flow all these
"Volichls," "Shers," "Jogs," "Bolgars," etc. I know also
that these *pseudo*-Jewish folksongs are direct borrow-
ings; they were not in the least transformed by the
Jewish melodic folk-genius, as Mr. Engel would have it.

A detail: Mr. Engel states that my example *Liuba-
vitcher Redl* as being chassidic with Polish traits does
not convince him; he has found in a collection of
Polish folk dances "not one melody of which the *Redl*
might be considered a rhythmic reiteration or variation."

I, too, see the difference between this *Redl* and the
Polish dances, as to their *literal* rhythmic structure.
But it is just as clear that this roundel contains all the
earmarks of the rhythmic accentuation of many Polish
dances: the pause followed by a syncopation, in the first
measure of the tune, the peculiar rhythmic configura-
tion of the fractions that form the second beat of the
second bar, etc. This air contains everything that
impresses our ear as definitely alien to Jewish song. Not
only the Polish folksong but also Chopin, so strongly
racial in his rhythmic traits, is shot through with these
peculiarities.[12]

[12] It is interesting to note that A. Z. Idelsohn, a prodigious collector
of the Jewish folksong, insists and illustrates with musical examples,
in his book on Jewish music (Chapter XVIII and Table XXVII) and

And mind you, this chassidic *Redl* is typical of the favorite, the widely spread kind of chassidic melody.

*   *   *

The second set of Mr. Engel's remarks tries to shell my contention that the originality of a great number of our popular domestic melodies and of the chassidic tunes of a similar type, is marred by a banal modal structure, by a pan-Oriental mode, so to speak. Mr. Engel points to the fact that a formidable number of domestic Jewish songs are built on other scales which do not use the Oriental interval of the augmented second; that in the *Sammelbuch* of the Petrograd Hebrew Folksong Society out of the sixty-two songs published, only twenty-two are built in the common Oriental mode.

True!   But a collection published in the initial, muddled stage of the new Jewish musical activity, when a banal air like *Eili, Eili* was considered the quintessence of Jewish music, a collection that contains songs flagrantly alien, such as the Ukrainian *Hob ich a por Ochsen* and the German *Schön binn ich, schön,* should not *now* serve as a basis for generalizing.   My own judgment is based on the immense new material of Jewish folksong gathered since the publication of the *Sammelbuch.*

However, the point most important in our dispute is this.   We have somehow developed a prejudiced, a

in his article published by the *Musical Quarterly* (October, 1932), that the Eastern Jewish folksong is greatly influenced by Polish and Ukrainian folk-music.   This is a blunt refutation of Mr. Engel's opinion.

very harmful idea that the Jewish song built in major
or in ordinary minor, in the Æolian or Dorian mode,
is not as typically Jewish, as melody molded in the common Oriental vein.

Neither do I take the modal traits of a song for a
deciding factor, when questioning its racial origin. The
mode is, however, symptomatic, and it explains much.

In this case, when I speak of the habitual structure
of the popular domestic and similar chassidic melos,
of their trite Oriental mode, I do it with a strong conviction that this kind of Jewish tune belongs mainly
to the racially muddy, wandering pan-Oriental chant.
This sort I have heard in profusion—by the Hungro-
Roumanian cabaret orchestras, by the native Armenian
bands of the Caucasus who played them on native
instruments, and by the Jewish *klezmorim,* folk-
musicians of the Bessarabian and Podolian villages in
Southern Russia.

Those who repudiate this kind of Jewish domestic
song are prompted by true æsthetic instinct and by
true racial taste. They sense a vagabond Oriental type,
a music vulgarly levelled not only in its modal nature
but in its very breath and diction.

*   *   *

The third group of Mr. Engel's objections pertains
to my finding that the racial response evoked by the
majority of the chassidic songs comes from their psychological content—the words, general import and emotional subsoil—and not from the national-melodic side.
Mr. Engel holds that my assertion is hypothetical; he

invites me to prove my ground by an analysis of the modal type of these songs and of their rhythmic accent. He also says: "That Mr. Saminsky's assertions are too sweeping, can be seen immediately. The impression given by the general import, the psychological subsoil and the verbal part, his argument of proof, constitutes a strange privilege of the domestic folksong. As if these factors are incapable of acting through the synagogal song: fancy the *Kol Nidre* in synagogal surroundings! Sometimes even a stranger thing is to be surmised: namely, that the chassidic *nigunim*—many of them without words, their strength lying only in their melody—act mainly through their verbal element."

In the pages of the general press, with no freedom to publish musical examples, it is rather difficult to debate points of modal analysis, to compare rhythmic types, etc. But it is fitting here to use the method of the ancient Hindu geometrician who writes above the design of his theorem, with its geometrical consequences evident: "Look!"

Take one of the emotionally strongest and most popular songs of Rabbi Levi Itzhak of Berditchev, *Dem Reben's Kaddish,* which Mr. Engel considers the best example of a chassidic melody. Detach yourself from its dramatic powerful verbal content; look it over and play or sing the melody without the words. Will the impression then remain unimpaired in strength, even though the general import of the song, its psychology, verbal and historical lining, stay with you subconsciously? Will this new impression approach, in character, in power, in definiteness of racial effect, any-

thing like the formidable reaction left by Levi Itzhak's
Kaddish when the latter is sung *with* words and *with*
the full awareness of its racial-psychological and historical import; when what I call the "general import of a
chassidic song" is given full sway?

Most assuredly, the impact of the song's psychology,
the effect of its word is not something owned by
domestic Jewish folk-music exclusively. The effect of
a synagogal canticle may also owe something or everything to the verbal part.

But all this is beside the point. What I meant by
insisting on the peculiar verbal impact of the domestic
folksong, is its ability to mislead us by screening its
alien melody with a smoke of racial psychological and
verbal effect.

The religious folksong is for manifest reasons incapable of this. It suffices to sing a racially crystalline
religious air, such as the Lithuanian *Omar Rabbi
Eliozor*,[13] with or without words, to perceive which is
the true Hebraic melodic style.

As to Mr. Engel's *reductio ad absurdum* angled out
of my argument,—that "in the chassidic *nigunim* without words there is an effect from the verbal part,"—I
do not even comprehend how such nonsense could be
implied. The subject of my argument was neither
dismembered, nor reduced to a single phenomenon. I
have quoted an entire range of qualities that cause the
emotional and racial action of the chassidic melody;
I did not speak of their verbal basis alone. And my

---

[13] This song is reproduced in the chapter "Music of the Russian
Orient" of my book *Music of Our Day.*

general argument pertained not only to chassidic tunes without words but also to the infinitely greater number of songs with words and, of course, to the ocean of domestic folksong.

* * *

Finally, I beg leave to state why it is rather difficult for me to remain calm and academic in this debate on the value of the popular type of our domestic song, why I am at times categoric, to the manifest displeasure of my esteemed opponent.

I am not a savant but a composer. I find it trying to remain a poised academic observer at a time when the very body of our Jewish music is being built up. I loath all the rickety tonal elements and the traits of racial neutrality, the well known traits of the vagabond pan-Oriental music which I perceive only too vividly in the inferior type of the chassidic melody and in many of our domestic *pseudo*-folksongs.

In this case, one cannot lean on the "dear to the Jewish heart" persuasion. This heart has mothered a vulgar musical comedy *Kune Lemel,* miserable *badchon* couplets and the Ukrainian *Hob ich a por Ochsen wos zey broken Loksen,* a song elevated to a high national position.

On the other hand, I do not altogether repudiate the national significance of even the trite domestic song or of the similar chassidic. They carry streams, even though diluted, of racial and national emotion or intonation, and play, therefore, a rôle in the building up of national music.

A Hebrew composer may be charmed by them, lured into fostering them, even while he is aware of their racial drabness.

But all this had place in the initial, chaotic stage of Jewish creative work.

In the present organic period, demolition is, in my opinion, just as important and valuable as is building up. My whole being, that of a worker in the Jewish musical field, revolts against the plea that in this domain "a place should be granted to everything and everybody."

The banal, the racially neutral, the muddy and rickety, the flagrantly borrowed element of our music, should be weeded out mercilessly from the cycle of means in use by our young creators. Otherwise this element is a source of feebleness and instability in our budding national-musical organism. And our young composition is doomed to a work nationally insignificant.

Engel did not respond to the above epistle. The matter was permitted to rest, until at a public convention in Moscow, after my paper on Hebrew music, another royal battle between Engel and myself ensued, a verbal debate this time. The general consensus of opinion held Engel defeated. He never again wrote on the matter. But a well known Petrograd writer, not a professional musician, writing under the name of *Unicus,* picked up the gauntlet and in an article *Vox profani* assaulted very forcefully some of my statements. His objections will be clearly seen from my reply.

Words of an Uninitiated
(A reply to Mr. Unicus)

The long controversy between Julius Engel and myself is not permitted by Mr. Unicus to end. He desires to interfere in his own right, that of a *profanus* and an "uninitiated."

A natural right Mr. Unicus uses somewhat too broadly. First, he reads Mr. Engel's and my argument none too attentively. Secondly, he oversimplifies a problem that has many subtle angles. He deduces the whole theorem to its initial stage, namely, to the sentimental sermon of yore: the depicting of the folksong as an appanage of the people because the people sing it, love it, express therein their joy, their woe.

That he reads Mr. Engel and myself somewhat too nonchalantly, may be perceived in the following words of Mr. Unicus, and in his supplication "not to brand our song as alien for the sole reason of an acquired feature or even alien origin."

"It seems to me," says Mr. *Unicus,* "that Mr. Saminsky has unwittingly pushed the problem off its proper place, with his remark that 'he knows where many chassidic songs, love songs, and wedding tunes come from.' . . ."

But, there is no pushing off the problem, in this assertion of mine.

Saying that I knew thoroughly the birthplace of these songs was in direct reply to Mr. Engel's testimony that having been born in Ukraine, he was witness to the fact that the Jewish folksong does not contain any appreciable Ukrainian element.

I, too, speak from an intimate knowledge of the region from which these melodies spring. But my assertions have a more direct bearing on the main center of the argument. I demolish with reason and proof; I "push off" nothing. My main contention is the difference in æsthetic value of the various types of folksong. I establish the existence of an elevated, original, well crystallized type, and that of a lowly, vagabond, common Oriental pattern to which chassidic melodies so often belong.

Mr. Unicus assures me that the presence of imitative traits in a folksong is not important. The presence of elements of Jewish folkspirit is the only thing to be considered as it transforms the borrowed tune effectively. Mr. Unicus breaks into an open door. For it was this writer who first brought out this point long ago. I also established the distinction between a direct borrowing, the one which does not grow into the body of the genuine folkmusic, and the real metamorphosis that gives a new life and a new nationality to an alien accretion.

I wrote, long ago, of the bar to the assimilation of an alien song set up in the national or racial melodic taste of a people. *Not every* alien song can be transmuted in the furnace of racial spirit; *not every* alien song can become *ours,* no matter how vigorously it rotates in Jewish quarters, even in the synagogue or chassidic milieu.

Der gilgul of a nigun, the metempsychosis of a tune,

does not consecrate all. "The arrogant accordeon tune that may have slipped into the synagogue service" will remain as repellent as before. It can only insult the synagogue. All this prattle about the consecration of an accordeon tune is a typical hyperbole of the "uninitiated."

What if a despicable factory chansonette *Oï Abram, ich kenn on dir nit zain* has slipped in and is adored by the Jewish town quarters of Odessa or Ekaterinoslav? Is this, too, a valuable "metamorphosis of a song"? Is something being consecrated here too?

To prove that these vagabond songs "branded" by me are irrevocably "ours" Mr. Unicus says:

> "Try to return the chassidic *nigun* to his first owner, to the Ukrainian or the Hungarian. Will he accept it? Will he recognize his seed?"

Indeed, try! Return the famous *Wolochl* to the Roumanians of Bukowina from where it has found its way to the chassidic service of Lioubavitch in Lithuania! Give back the *Makarower Nigun* to the White Russian peasant whose warm kinsman this tune manifestly is! Try to hand back some of the loveliest *freilichs,* joyous wedding songs, and *jogs* (roundels) to the Moldovans of the village of Vale Hotzulovo in the Kherson district of Southern Russia, where I have heard them; or the *bolgars* and *shers,* to the Bulgarians of the Bender and Ismail villages of southern Bessarabia, where they gladden not exclusively Jewish weddings! Try to return the favorite children's song *Hob ich a por Ochsen wos sie broken Loksen,* "My yoke of oxen likes noodles," to the Ukrainians, and *Schön binn ich, schön* to the Bessarabian or Volynian Germans! And do not think that all these races will repudiate these songs as alien!

Mr. Unicus insists that only *"where* the song is headed" matters, not *"whence* it comes." His is only half of the idea, for "where" depends upon "from whence." The worthlessness of the melody of the vagabond type, of the lowly kind of domestic and chassidic music lies in its basic melodic neutrality: this music does not arrive anywhere because melodically it comes from "nowhere," as far as the Jewish racial taste and folk-creation perceive it.

*   *   *

Were these pointed problems of Hebrew art of an academic significance only, one could take much less to heart the naïve simplifying of questions, the lack of discernment in the national and aesthetic valuation of the various song types, the dissertations typical of the "uninitiated."

As a matter of fact, we are offered an art policy: not to ostracize this or another type of Jewish folksong for its alien features, even for an alien origin.

Mr. Unicus' soliloquies are linked to typical "profane" truisms that "the people sing this song, it is permeated with their joy and sorrow; it is therefore the people's song." This means to continue, to even bless the policy of *laissez faire, laissez passer,* "let nature take its course," in Jewish music, a policy already responsible for the mire of assimilation and neutralizing in which Jewish musical creation is sunk.

Where then lies the essence and the power of national gravitation in art if not in the will to freedom of the creative flame, if not in the clearing of every channel of the national spirit from worthless alien sediment, from borrowed *pasticcio* that distorts the growth of the golden wheat of racial creation?

Given these barriers to a correct growth of Hebrew musical culture, *tertium non datur;* a third outlet does not exist.

One must either deem original Jewish music non-existent and impossible, or accept the peculiarity of its life. But, if the original Jewish music exists and can be extricated, one is bound to accept the travail of cleansing; the analysis of all types of melodic folk-creation and the scale of their racial worth and purity; the distinction between blunt borrowing of alien melos and its true metamorphosis in the Jewish sense. To the battle *ad majorem gloriam* of the purest type of our folk-melos which is and will be pursued by a Jewish musician of strong convictions, one must be reconciled.

FINALE: On Hebraic and Judaic Music

It is easy to perceive how this whole diatribe can be usefully applied to the problems of any young and growing racial or national culture, the American, for example. In this debate, replace the native elements borrowed by the Jews—Polish, Roumanian, Ukrainian, —by the Negro and Indian folksong assimilated by the Americans; substitute the elevated, oldest and genuine American song of the Anglo-Celtic type for the highest Hebraic melos. Then the whole problem of American folk-music as a basis for an original American culture, will be traced in all its phases and detail.

However, as it would be irrelevant here to go into this field, I shall confine this *finale* to one more important attack on my theoretical earthwork.

A gifted Paris musician, composer and writer, Léon Algasi, answered in the Paris press an article of mine, also published in Paris.

"Biblical music! This is the first time that we encounter this expression penned by a musician. And we ask whether or not 'biblical music' corresponds to reality, whether it is not a term of convenience which an eminent musician and an adroit writer—M. Lazare Saminsky—employs for the necessities of his cause."

But, M. Algasi adds, that he does not reproach me for the use of the term "biblical" in the same sense as

"Hebraic," for applying it to the traditional synagogal melos and the cantillation of the Bible. He objects only to the opposing of the Hebraic element to the idiom born in the ghetto in a relatively recent epoch.

But, alas, M. Algasi's argument either repeats the old aria that the "national genius puts its marks on the assimilated elements and naturalizes them"; or bases its conclusions on incomplete induction making a limited use of the existing facts, too limited to warrant a generalization. Thus, for instance, he insists that the famous sephardic *Kaddish,* the one harmonized by Ravel, cannot be called Hebraic with assurance as its mode is not that of the Bible, of our religious tradition.

It is only too evident that M. Algasi knows a too scant list of examples of biblical cantillation, probably only those of the southern French, the Carpentras tradition.

At any rate, the profusion of facts and historical detail presented in this book, I dare say, uphold the naturalness of my distinction between the Hebraic and the Judaic in music, and the legitimacy of the distinction as well.

INDEX

Aavo rabo mode, 32-34

Achron, Joseph, 48, 51; *Stempenyou,* 66, 137; genius and work, 135-137; *Canzonetta,* 135; *Violin Concerto,* 136; *Adon Olam,* 137; violin pieces, 229

Adler, Cyrus, 20n

Adon Olam, settings by various composers, 172

Adonoy Moloch mode, 30-2; Ashkenazic chant, 26, 31

Aeolian mode, 18; Aeolian *Mogen Ovos,* 24-30, 35

Akiba, Rabbi, 20, 21, 199

Algasi, Léon, 50, 253-4

Ambrose, Bishop of Milan, 30, 214; Ambrosian chant, 210, 217, 220

Ancient trumpet calls, *tekia, terua,* 19

Anglo-Celtic song, 121

Artaxerxes I, King of Persia, 21

Ashkenazic song, 26 (ex. 2, 3), 61

A solis ortu, ancient canticle, 22

Av harachmim, prayer, 46-7

Avoda service, 25

Baal Shem, 40

Bach, Sebastian, 174, 222

Bachur, Eliahu, 204-5

Bacon, Francis, quoted, 38

Badchon, 71, 71n

Babylonian captivity, 21

Babylonian Jews, sacred chants, 13, 14, 15, 21, 60, 204; musical tradition, 214

Baron Guinsbourg's Expedition, 22n, 46, 51, 59; collecting

Georgian Hebrew chants, 147, 149

Beethoven, *Quartet,* 3; *Hymn to Joy,* 10; *Ruins of Athens,* 29; *E-sharp minor Quartet,* 30; link with Viennese Hebrew community, 30; *Ninth Symphony,* 32

Beimel, Jacob, 168, 181

Beltzer, Nissan, life and work, 46-7; *Hayom haras olam,* 47 (ex. 28), 234, 236

Benjamin of Tudela, Rabbi, 13, 58, 156

Binder, A. W., 77n, 168

Birnbaum, Edward, 31

Blitzstein, Marc, opera *Caïn,* 127; compared to Schoenberg, 127

Bloch, Ernest, 8, 9, 48; *Shelomo,* 66; *Israel* symphony, 68; genius and work, 112, 116-8; the best Bloch, 117-8; *Sacred Service,* 176-180

Borodin, 29

Brahms, finale of the *First Symphony,* 10

Brandes, Georg, quoted, 68

Breslauer, Emil, 30n

Byron, Lord, on Beau Brummell's dress, 123

Cabalists, 40, 132-3

Caesar, *De bello gallico,* Georgians compared to Gauls, 147

Cantica, 22

Cantillation of the Bible, 21; its modes, 24-35; cantillation of the

Cantillation of the Bible (Cont'd.) Pentateuch, 30-1; historical survey and analysis of, 195-223; chanting of the Prophets, 202-3

Carmen Sylva, Queen of Rumania, 159

Castelnuovo Tedesco, *Dance of King David*, 69

Caucasian Jews, sacred chants, 13; Georgian *Shir hashirim*, 14, 15; Georgian Kaddish, 16, 25, 59; ethnological and musical analysis of chants, 59-60, 149-151; illustrations, 151 (ex. 1), 15, (ex. 2), 16 (ex. 7); influence of Persian music, 154; historical data concerning Caucasian Jews, 154-156

Chamberlain, Stewart Houston, 75, 104; on Heine, 105

Champagne, old Jewish settlements, 35, 61

Chanler, Theodore, quoted, 122

Chant des trouvères, 36

Charlemagne, Emperor, 20, 210, 217

Chassidism, 36, 40, 41; chassidic song, 41-3, 238-247

Chazzanuth, 23; *chazzan*, medieval picture of, 181

Cheironomony, 195, 196, 197, 208

Chesterton, G. K., quoted, 7

Citkowitz, Israel, 125, 127

Classics of the synagogue, 45-6

Codex Alexandrinus, 22

Cohen, Rabbi Francis, quoted, 211

Constantinople, 143, 158; the chief rabbi, Haïm Bejarano, 158; *B'nai Brith* lodge, 159

Copland, Aaron, 122-5; *Vitebsk*, 122; *Concerto*, 124; *Music for the Theatre*, 124

Cornill, Carl Heinrich, 19n

Coussemaker, Edmond, quoted, 200

Cowell, Henry, 122n, 126, 231n

Crusades, 47, 60-1, 212

Davison, Arichibald T., quoted, 173; quoted, 175

Debussy, 51

DeSola, D. A., quoted, 213

Dom Gatard, quoted, 200, 215-6; quoted, 217, 220

Dom Pothier, Joseph, quoted, 209, 214

Dzimitrovski, Abram, 50

East European Hebrew musician, his plight, 5; populist wing, 53

Egidio, Cardinal, 205

El Greco, 94, 161

Eli Zion, old chant, 34

Emanuel of Rome, 181

Enelow, H. G., 19n; quoted, 207

Engel, Carl, 97

Engel, Julius, 48, 51, 227, 231; quoted, 232, 237, 238; polemic with L. Saminsky on the originality and value of the chassidic song, 238-47

Ewen, David, 36

En Kelohenu, origin, 170

Ezra the Scribe, 21, 198, 199

Fleischer, Oscar, author of *Neumen Studien*, 197, 207, 218 (on the Lament of Jeremiah)

Friedlander, Arthur, 208

Friedmann, Aaron, 34n, 35n

Gatti, Guido, quoted, 118

Gershwin, George, 119-22; *Rhapsody in Blue*, 122; *Concerto in F*, 122

Gerovitch, Eliezer, 46; life and work, 181-191

Geshem, ancient prayer, 14, 16 (ex. 4)

Gilman, Lawrence, quoted, 34, 120, 124

Glinka, Russian composer, 149; his opera *Russlan and Lioudmila*, 149

Gniéssin, Michael, 48, 49, 51; *Rachel's Tomb*, 66; on the Jewishness of Wagner, 98-9, 100; life, genius and work, 128-33; *Prelude* to Shelley's "Prometheus," 130; *Hymn to the Pest*, 130, 131; *Snowflakes*, 131; *Celestial Dew*, 132; ideas on the synagogue and its music, 186-8, 189; his *Nigun*, 230

Gobineau, Artur, 104

Goldberg, Isaac, quoted, 108, 120

Golem, 115

Gonzaga, Dukes of Mantua, 166

Gregorian chant, 22, 61, 62

Gregorian church modes, Phrygian 32; Doric, 163; similarity to Hebrew chant, 214

Gregory, the Great, Pope, 30, 216

Gruenberg, Louis, 8; genius and work, 112-15; *Emperor Jones*, 114

Guido d'Arezzo, 195, 214

Handel, *Maccabeans*, 172

Hanukkah, 170

Hebraïc idiom, 66-7, 70

Hebrew accentuation, 201

Hebrew colleges in Bagdad (12th century), 13

Hebrew Folksong Society in Petrograd, 49-50, 188, 228-9

Heifetz, Jascha, 109, 110

Henderson, W. J., quoted, 9

Henry, Leigh, quoted, 116; on Ernest Bloch, 179-80

High Holidays, 22

High Priest, 25

Idelsohn, A. Z., 14n, 19n, 20n, 181, 241n

Irish culture, 108, 198n; language, 207

Isaiah, Prophet, 62, 206

Isidore of Seville, Bishop, quoted, 208-9, 220

Iste Confessor, ancient canticle, 22, 170

Italian-Hebrew synagogal music, 164-5

Jacobi, Frederick, 125-6; *Sabbath Evening Service*, 125-6; *Concerto for cello and orchestra*, 126; *String Quartet*, 126

Jeremiah, Prophet, his *Lament*, 218-9

Jerome, Saint, editor of the *Vulgata*, 217-8

Jesus Christ, 94, 206-7

Jewish aristocrats, their worship, 7

Jewish folksong, collecting of, 48; gathering of Georgian Hebrew chants, 147-9; facts and polemic on, 227-54; song collecting in Russia, 229; originality and value of the chassidic song, 238-47

Jewishness in music, 75-7

Jewish musical tradition, 18, 19, 20; historic tendencies, 53-4; continuity of Hebrew melos, 61-2

Jewish national music, 65

Johnson, Samuel, quoted, 125

Julius II., Pope, 159

Judaïc idiom, 67-8, 70, 235

Kaddish, prayer for the dead, 34; Sephardic *Kaddish*, 35

Kalonymos, Rabbi Meshullam ben, 37; creator of *piyutim*, 161

Karo, Rabbi Joseph, author of the *Shulchan Aruch,* 35
Kedusha, 172, 175
Kings, of Judea, 155; of Samaria, 155; of Persia, 156; of Georgia, 155; of Lombardy, 216
Knesses haggedolo (The Great Assembly) and its members, 198
Kohler, Kaufmann, quoted, 19, 188
Kol Nidre, 3, 35
Krein, Alexander, 48, 51; *Ghazelen,* 66, 69; genius and work, 133-5; *Hebrew suite,* 134; *Salomé,* 134

Lasso, Orlando, 222
Laudate Zion, 34n
Leo X dei Medici, 165
Levandowski, Louis, *Unsane Tokef,* 36; as synagogal composer, 45; *Ki keshimcho,* 45
Levi, Rabbi Itzhak, 41; his *Kaddish,* 42-3, 234, 235, 236, 244-5
Levites, 19, 220
Liszt, Franz, 49; impression of Sulzer, quoted, 49, 75; on Jewish musicians, 107-8
Luther, Martin, 14; hymn, *Eine Feste Burg,* 14; in the synagogue, 170

Macaulay, Thomas, quoted, 106
Malory, Sir Thomas, *Le Morte d'Arthur,* 102
Maggid, David, authority on biblical cantillation, 200n; quoted, 205-6
Magrepha, 19
Maharil, Rabbi Jacob Levi Mölin, 181
Mahler, Gustav, 8, 91, 95
Marcello, Benedetto, 29, 165
Mayence, scenes of Jewish martyrdom, 38

Mendel, Arthur, on Gregorian music, quoted, 210n
Mendelssohn, Felix, 44; *Lied ohne Worte* in b-minor, 44; *Scottish Symphony,* 44; post-classical style, 75; *Lorelei,* 81; *Meerestille und glückliche Fahrt,* 81; life, genius, work and drama, 81-2, 86-7; *Psalm XLII,* 222
Mendoza y Bovadilla, Cardinal, 96
Meyerbeer, 29, 29n, 44; *Prophet,* 44; *The Huguenots,* 83; life, work, genius and drama, 83-8
Mi Chomocho, 22; traditional, 170
Middle Ages, Jewish music of, 23-4, 31, 36, 39, 222
Milhaud, Darius, 53, 91, 95
Milner, Moses, *Unsane Tokef,* 36, 66; participant in Jewish musical renaissance, 48; *El hatzipor,* 62; *In Cheider,* 71; genius and work, 138-9; *Songs,* 139; *In Cheider,* 230
Mimicry of modernism, 9
Mixolydian mode, in Hebrew music, 30, 31, 32, 61
Minnesong, 31, 36, 61
Mogen Ovos mode, 18, 24-30
Monteverdi, Claudio, 166, 186
Moore, George F., quoted, 53
Moslem chant, 33; influence of, 35, 36, 61
Moussorgski, *Joshua,* 5, 238
Mozart, 174, 176

Nachman of Bratzlav, Rabbi, 42
Naumann, Emil, 22n
Naumburg, Samuel, 45; *Adonay, Adonay,* 45, 234
Neginoth, 21
Negro spirituals, 121
Nehemiah, Governor of Judea, 21, 198
Neumes, 21, 195, 200; spiritual affinities, 207

New Era, its influence on Hebrew music, 38-9, 44, 222
Newman, Ernest, quoted, 97 (on Wagner's Jewishness), quoted, 98
Nietzsche, Friedrich, quoted, 4

Olenu, old chant, 60-1
Ornstein, Leo, 118-9

Palazzo Uffizi, 159
Palestine, rôle in Hebrew music, 77; land of Chalutzim tunes, 77
Palestinian folksong, 34
Palestrina, *Psalm 42*, 222
Paris, Great Synagogue, 20
Paul the Deacon, 22, 170
Pedro the Cruel, King of Castile, 161
Pentateuch, chanting of, 19, 202-3, 214, 221
Persian Jews, 21
Peter the Glutton, his *Historia Scholastica*, 212
Pisk, Paul, 53
Pius X, Pope, his *Motu Propriu*, 173; restoration of the Gregorian chant, 173, 220
Piyutim, synagogal poems, 35-6; author of Saadia Gaon, Meshullam ben Kalonymos, Jehuda Halevi, etc., 161-2
Plain-chant, 61, 215, 220
Polish influence, 228, 235, 239, 240, 241
Polo, Marco, 3, 13n
Prince of Captivity, 156
Prunières, Henri, 166n, 186
Psalms, ancient manner of rendition, *Hallel*, 20
Purcell, *Hallelujah*, 172

Raphael, portrait of Pope Julius II, 159; portraits of Jewish musicians, 165

Rashi, 196
Ravel, 35
Reis, Claire, 112n
Renaissance, 47; in Jewish music, 48
Renan, Ernest, 159, 212
Responses, ancient, 20
Reuchlin, Joseph, 214
Rhineland, old Jewish settlements, 18, 35; massacre, 47, 61; sacred chants of, 204, 214
Rimski-Korsakov, 49, 75
Rock of Ages, origin, 170
Rogers, Bernard, 126
Rosenfeld, Paul, quoted, 116; quoted, 119
Rosh Hashanah, music, 19, 31
Rosovski, Salomo, 49, 51; his work on biblical cantillation, 202; *Trio*, 230
Rossi, Salamone, 166; his *Adon Olam*, 166; his friendship with Monteverdi, 166, 172
Rousseau, Jean Jacques, quoted, 124
Rubinstein, Anton, 44; *Persian Songs*, 44; post-classical style, 75; life, genius, work and drama, 89-91
Rumanian influence, 33, 235, 240

Sabanéyev, Leonide, quoted, 109; quoted, 134
Saint Gall and his monastery, 198
Saleski, Gdal, 98
Salonica, 158; the Chief Rabbi, Jacob Meïr, 159
Saminsky, Lazare, 14n; *Rachel*, 18; *V'shamru*, 32; *Sabbath Evening Service*, 32n; *Music of Our Day*, 33n; *The Great Rabbis' Invocation*, 41; *Ten Hebrew Folksongs and Folkdances*, 42n; opera-ballet, *The Vision of Ariel*, 47; on historic flow of Hebrew melos, 55-6 (quota-

Saminsky, Lazare (Contd.) tion); on racial melodic taste, 56-7 (quotation); on creative and religious phenomena of racial order, 72-3 (quotation); lecture in Constantinople, 159

Saminsky, Lillian, *Poems and Adaptations*, 131n

Sanborn, Pitts, quoted, 38, 94

Schechter, Solomon, quoted, 43; quoted, 115

Schloezer, Boris, quoted, 91-2

Schoenberg, Arnold, 8, 91, 93-4

Schorr, Baruch, *Yaale*, 46 (ex. 28)

Schumann, Robert, 87; on Meyerbeer, 87

Sessions, Roger, quoted, 117

Seville, Cathedral of, 178

Sh'ma Israel, 19, 21; ancient Georgian-Persian, 151 (illustrated, 16, ex. 5), 220

Shneur Zalman, Rabbi, 41-2

Shofar, 19

Silluk, 202

Slonimsky, Nicolas, quoted, 94; quoted, 231

Soferim (the Scribes), 198-99

Spanish-Hebrew songs, 160-5; musical illustrations, 151 (ex. 3), 152 (ex. 4, 5); old Castillian *romanzas*, 160; the *Selichot*, 162; Aragonese ballads, 163-4; biblical chants, 204

Spicker, Max, 172, 175

Streicher, Lioubov, her *Song of Songs*, 230

Synagogal song, its modes, 24-35; American synagogue music, 168-175; oldest traditional melodies, 171; would be traditional chants, 171

Sulzer, Solomon, 45; *En komocho*, 45; his singing, 49, 170; influence of, 183, 234

Taamim, 21

Talmud, talmudists, 19; *Mishnah*, 22-3; passages concerning the biblical cantillation, 199; concerning cheironomy, 206

Tannaim, their age, 22

Te Deum Laudamus, 3, 214

Temple Emanu-El, New York, 20; its Choir Committee and sponsoring of new religious compositions, 125n, 137n; type of hymns used, 174; its cantor, Moshe Rudinov, 181

Temple of Jerusalem, ancient ceremonial, 18, 19, 21, 25

Thal, ancient melody, 14, 16 (ex. 4), 25

Tiflis, synagogues of, 143-7; types of worshipers, 144-6; Dagestan Jews, 144; prayer-manner, 145; Georgian *chachams*, 148; sacred chants used, 149-51; illustrations, 151 (ex. 1), 15 (ex. 2), 16 (ex. 7)

Thompson, Oscar, quoted, 227

Toledo, the builder of the future El Greco house, Samuel Halevi, 161

Toye, Francis, quoted, 100

Tragedy of the Jewish composer, 5

Treves, Rabbi Hertz, 181; quoted, 182

Turkey, Sephardim of, 158; their leaders, 159-60; their Spanish-Hebrew poetry and music, 160-65; musical illustrations, 151 (ex. 3), 152 (ex. 4, 5), the *Selichot*, 162

Ukrainian influence, 228, 233, 239, 240, 242

Universal Forum, 10, 223

Unsane Tokef, 36-7

Vallas, Léon, 51
Vay'chulu hashomaim, traditional chant, 26 (ex. 2), 29; traces of in Meyerbeer's work, 44
Vecchi Orazio, his *Amphiparnasso,* 167
Venice, 29, 166; shelter of friends and defamers of Jewish music, 167; Palazzo Vendramin, 167; St. Marc's Cathedral, 186
V'hakkohanim, 25
Viennese Hebrew community, 30
Vinaver, Eugène, 102n
V'shamru, 31-2; traces of in Meyerbeer's work, 44

Wagner, Peter, 22n, 209n; quoted, 210
Wagner, Richard, 75; the Jewishness of, 96-107; *Tristan,* 101-3; use of Celtic legends, 101-3; overemphasis in *Die Walküre,*

103; dying guest at the Palazzo Vendramin, 167, 170
Wandering scale, 33
Warburg, Gerald F., American musician, sponsor of Ernest Bloch's service, 176n
Wassermann, Jacob, quoted, 66
Western Hebrew musician, his plight, 5; radical wing, 52-3
Wilson, Woodrow, defending the best Protestant music, 173
Wise, Rabbi Isaac M., quoted, 62

Yasser, Joseph, 168, 203
Yemenite Jews, sacred chants, 13, 14, 15, 21, 30n; their appearance and habits compared to those of the Georgian Jews, 158
Yom Kippur, 31; music used in American synagogues, 170, 175

Zechariah, Prophet, 214
Zionist movement, influence, 48